SOCIALISM

Politics

Editor

PROFESSOR W. A. ROBSON
B.SC (ECON), PH.D, LL.M
Professor Emeritus of Public Administration
in the University of London

SOCIALISM

A SHORT HISTORY

Norman MacKenzie
B.SC(ECON)
Lecturer in Sociology in the University of Sussex

HUTCHINSON UNIVERSITY LIBRARY
LONDON

HUTCHINSON & CO *(Publishers)* LTD
178–202 Great Portland Street, London W1

London Melbourne Sydney
Auckland Bombay Toronto
Johannesburg New York

First published 1949
Second (revised) edition May 1966
Reprint March 1967

This book has been set in Times, printed in Great Britain
on Smooth Wove paper by Anchor Press, and
bound by Wm. Brendon, both of Tiptree, Essex

For

John Oakley

Drongen: May 1944

CONTENTS

FOREWORD

This is a revised edition of a book first published in 1949. Events since then have made it desirable to substitute new chapters for those that appeared originally as chapters 1, 15, and 16, but only minor textual changes have been made elsewhere. Since 1949, moreover, the development of paperback publishing has made it possible to drop the original bibliography—many titles in which have become difficult to procure—and to supply in its place a shorter list of books for further reading, all of which are available in Britain and the United States in paperback editions. The original purpose of the book remains. It was not written to provide a definitive history of socialist ideas and movements, for such a task could not be accomplished in so limited a space. It was designed to offer an introductory volume from which the reader could go on to more detailed or specialist studies.

N.M.

I

A NEW VIEW OF SOCIETY

At the end of the eighteenth century, two momentous changes took place in Europe. The first was political: the French Revolution dramatically asserted the rights of man to liberty, equality and fraternity. The second was economic: new technical inventions, harnessed to the steam-engine, quickly promoted an industrial revolution. Together, they produced the capitalist system, a bourgeois order based upon political liberty, formal equality before the law, private ownership of the means of production, and free competition in the market. But the very changes which created this new society provided the basis for criticising it. The slogans of democracy, originally directed against feudal privilege, could as well be turned against inequalities that arose from acquired wealth. The idea of solidarity (or fraternity) could be opposed to the competitive ethos of liberal individualism. The principle of common political action could easily be extended, by the working class that was being formed by the factory system, to common industrial action against the employers. By the third decade of the nineteenth century, the essential features of industrial capitalism had been established in Britain; but, at the same time, the political and economic conditions that had made this possible had also made it possible to conceive of an alternative view of society—what we now call socialism.

A New View of Society, indeed, was the title of one of the earliest pamphlets which set out such an alternative. Its author, Robert Dale Owen, was a successful but radically-minded manufacturer, who had become convinced that human needs could best be satisfied by a combination of political democracy and the common ownership of industry which he called co-operation. The first use of the word 'socialism' actually occurred in an Owenite publication, the *Cooperative Magazine*, in 1827; for several years thereafter no clear distinction was made between 'socialism', co-operation', 'radical democracy' or even 'communism'. All these terms were loosely used for any system of ideas which was politically radical and socially collectivist.

Even today the word 'socialist' has many meanings. It may be used, for instance, by members of the British Labour Party to describe their programme of moderate social reform; or by Soviet communists to characterise the present stage of development of the USSR; or by Israelis talking about a *kibbutz*, or co-operative farm. But unless the term is to lose all pretence at precision, becoming merged at one extreme with any form of democratic reform and at the other extreme with all types of totalitarian state control, it must refer to certain ideas about the nature of society and the ways in which it can be changed. A liberal democrat in the United States, for example, may argue for a publicly-sponsored health service; but such a reform would be no more socialist than the provision of public education or a national postal system. In wartime, an English conservative could support many kinds of state action which, in time of peace, he would oppose as destructive of personal initiative and private property rights. Nazi Germany had many collectivist features, but despite the name, 'National Socialism', no one would seriously propose including the Hitler regime in a study of socialism simply because there was highly centralised control of the political and economic system. Some aspects of socialism, certainly, are akin to utilitarian reformism, as others are to authoritarianism; but as the term has been employed by various social movements in the nineteenth and twentieth centuries it implies a distinct group of doctrines which it may be helpful to summarise at the outset of this book.

Every socialist theory implies a moral criticism of the existing social order, and opposes to it a conception of a society free from injustice and the strictures of inequality. Whether the system that is attacked is a modern bourgeois democracy, such as contemporary Britain or America, or a colonialist regime such as those that Britain, France and Holland maintained until after World War II, or a society based on racial segregation, such as South Africa, the socialist critique focusses upon its denial of human equality. Even though much of Marx's writing was devoted to proving, by the logic of 'scientific socialism', that the capitalist system was ultimately doomed, the pages of *Capital* echo with phrases of great moral fervour as he declaims against its denial of essential human rights. Other socialist theories, especially in Britain where religious dissent played an important role in shaping the ideas of the emergent labour movement, draw more upon Christian morality for their arguments against the present system and their vision of the New Jerusalem of human brotherhood that could take its place.

Socialism, moreover, assumes the perfectibility of man. If the failings of a social system are attributed to the failings of human nature, there is clearly little hope of any useful or enduring reform. But if the defects stem, not from man, but from the institutions whereby he is governed, then man may achieve freedom by changing these institutions. The socialist must thus take an optimistic view of men's capacity to live in fraternity and to co-operate to mutual advantage. From such assumptions it follows that the socialist is prone to attribute war and crime, economic failure, poverty, illiteracy and ill-health to the shortcomings of the social system, and to insist that some different form of social organisation will eliminate these evils.

It is not enough to diagnose what is wrong: it is also necessary to believe that change is possible. There have been many social critics who have been dissatisfied with the system under which they have lived, but who have seen no practical means by which it might be changed for the better. It is in such circumstances that utopian ideas have flourished. The description of an imaginary society serves as an effective contrast to present ills, but the essence of all utopias is that they provide no map by which the fable island of the blessed can be found. It is only since the rise of modern industry, which seems to offer both the possibility of material abundance and, in the organised working class, a revolutionary instrument for achieving it, that socialist ideas have moved out of the utopian phase into that of practical politics. Every socialist theory, therefore, must include a programme of action—whether it relies on trade unionism, co-operation, a mass political party, a revolutionary conspiracy, or guerilla warfare.

Finally, there must be a will to change. A socialist theory may offer a moral criticism of society; it may analyse its material defects; it may propose an alternative form of political and economic organisation; it may suggest practical means by which the change can be accomplished. All of these together are the essence of any socialist ideology. But it will not make headway unless large masses of people are prepared to accept it. Early socialist writers did not take much account of this fact: their new view of society seemed so rational, so self-evidently desirable, that they often assumed that little more than good publicity was needed to win the support of all men of goodwill. But Marx, and all later Marxists, put great emphasis on what Marx called the 'material preconditions' of change; unless the time was ripe, all the advocacy in the world would not move masses of men into action. However, Marx insisted, there would be a widespread desire for change once the appropriate conditions were fulfilled. Capitalism must have exhausted its potential for productive development, so that men could clearly see the need for replacing it; the society must be shaken by war, economic crisis, or some other form of social breakdown; and there must be present both an effective socialist theory and an organised socialist movement capable of providing leadership to the potentially revolutionary masses.

The substance of these general ideas would be accepted by most of those who call themselves socialists. The differences begin when any attempt is made to apply them in practice—differences that account for many of the controversies among socialists and the schisms within socialist organisations which are described in this book. When (simply to take the last point) are conditions ripe for the transformation of capitalist society? When industry has developed, and there is a large and militant working class? Or when industry is still an unimportant factor, but there is a powerful nationalist movement and—because a colonial regime is breaking down—it is possible for a relatively small revolutionary group to take power? Such questions are not academic: they have been one of the focal points of dispute among Marxists since the death of Marx, and in modern times they have been shifted out of the realm of sectarian dispute and on to the world stage. The issue is no longer (as it was in the period when the tiny Marxist movement in Russia split into Bolshevik and Menshevik factions) one of party doctrine. It underlies the antagonism between the Soviet and Chinese communists, and also the sharp doctrinal struggle now going on between communists in all the advanced countries and those in the former colonial areas of Asia, Africa and Latin America.

This controversy, in fact, enables us to look at the history of the socialist movement in a new perspective. Until quite recently it was easy to assume that socialism as an idea and as a movement was closely linked to the emergence of industrial capitalism, and to the possibility of transforming it into a socialist system. This was the central idea of classical Marxism, and it was shared to a greater or lesser extent by socialists of many persuasions. While mass socialist organisations (including the communist movement) were largely confined to advanced industrial countries, this belief seemed logical and convincing. The one significant exception—the fact that the first successful Marxist revolution took place neither in England nor Germany, but in backward Russia—took a great deal of explaining. It was necessary for Lenin to make substantial revisions of classical Marxism in order to account for his success, and even when the Bolshevik revolution had been accomplished he still regarded it as something of a happy accident which could only be the prelude to socialist revolutions in the more advanced states of Western Europe. His colleague, Leon Trotsky, took the point so seriously that he came to believe that the Soviet system could not become socialist unless it served as the base for extending the world revolution—and thus came into conflict with Josef Stalin's doctrine that socialism could be built in one country, even one where the bourgeois revolution had been so feeble and industry was so undeveloped as Russia.

Since the end of World War II, however, the picture has changed. Apart from the communist countries of East Europe (themselves backward, with large peasant populations, and subject to post-war

Soviet occupation), no real headway has been made by revolutionary Marxism in Europe. The French and Italian communist parties are both large, but both are isolated and have no prospect of taking power. But the story is different in Asia, and may well be different in Africa and Latin America—as the Cuban example has shown. Communism is a militant and successful creed in such places: China is the notable instance, where the communist régime has come close to reviving the revolutionary doctrines of Trotsky, but Indonesia, India and Vietnam are all cases in point. They are all cases, moreover, where none of Marx's original conditions are present. There has been no real bourgeois revolution in these former colonial states. The nearest parallel has been the struggle for national independence and the creation of weak new régimes. There has been little development of industry; and one cannot really speak of a significant working class. They are all essentially poor, agrarian societies, in which the landlord and the usurer are the exploiters, not the capitalist.

Yet, if we disregard the reforms made by social-democratic parties in Britain, Scandinavia and Australasia, these societies have seen the only dramatic advance in recent years of movements claiming lineage from classical nineteenth-century socialism. Why should this be so? And what conclusions can we draw from this fact?

A partial explanation may lie in the fact that the social systems of these new nations are much more ramshackle than those of complex industrial societies. There are no highly developed administrative structures, no elaborate patterns of work, no strong political traditions, no social security provisions nor widespread education. On the contrary, these regimes have scarcely involved the mass of the people, who live in illiteracy and poverty. Their conditions of life are much closer to those of European peasants in the earliest years of industrialisation than they are to those of the modern working-class. In these societies, moreover, there have been great changes: old colonial régimes have gone, often under strong pressure and even after armed insurrection by nationalist movements. They are, therefore, unstable societies, which are peculiarly vulnerable to pressure from without and disruption from within.

Yet this is not sufficient reason for the spread of revolutionary movements in the under-developed countries, though it may partially account for their success. These movements, which call themselves Marxist even though they cannot be fitted into the classical Marxist pattern, have one major characteristic in common. They are all fundamentally peasant revolutions, based upon the villages rather than the towns, and using guerilla tactics rather than classical revolutionary techniques to establish themselves. This fact may provide a clue. Though when such movements gain power, as in China, their leaders may seek to industrialise the economy, and thereby create the working-class which Marx regarded as the vital condition for the building of a socialist society, it is significant that the real revolutionary drive comes from the countryside, and that its most effective rallying-point is the slogan of land reform. The peasant, armed with an automatic weapon, fights for the land: all other objectives are secondary.

We can see this demonstrated clearly in the history of Chinese communism, and in other agrarian movements led by communists today. But a backward glance reveals that a similar pattern underlay the Bolshevik revolution. Its slogan was 'Land, Bread and Peace', and its success depended upon the fact that the peasant masses were tired of war and wanted land: the proletarian uprisings in Petrograd and Moscow may have been the decisive actions (copied from the successive *coups d'état* in France), but without peasant support they would have collapsed. Lenin's nominal purpose was to use the proletariat to carry out Russia's long-delayed bourgeois revolution, and to move directly thereafter to establish a socialist society. This was the theory of 'the permanent revolution'. His actual achievement was to mobilise a peasant majority to install a proletarian dictatorship, which then attempted to make the social and economic development of Russia square with Marxist predictions.

It is, therefore, worth asking whether there is any important case where Marx's original model of a revolutionary proletariat taking power has worked. The short answer is that there is not. There have been abortive attempts to make it work, in Germany after World War I for example, but none succeeded. It may be worth asking a further question. Has any major social revolution occurred that did not have the ownership of the land as one of its foremost issues? A strong case can be made that the underlying struggle in the English

Civil War was the ownership and use of the land; this was certainly a decisive element in the French Revolution; it is present both in the American War of Independence and in the American Civil War. It has been a vital component in the Yugoslav revolution, in Cuba, and elsewhere.

We cannot analyse this matter at length here, though we shall return to it in the last chapters of this book. But it must be raised at the outset precisely because it bears so directly upon the fundamental assumptions made by most nineteenth-century socialists, and because it is so directly related to the tactics of reform or revolution which they debated at such length. One of the fascinating ironies of modern history lies in the fact that an idea so closely linked to industrialism, and a movement so based upon the growth of a working-class, should be inherited by a peasantry in arms.

2

THE BIRTH OF AN IDEA

Where does the history of socialism begin? Both the political doctrine and the mass labour organisations, in their familiar and modern form, are essentially the product of the nineteenth century. They began, early in the industrial age, as a protest against the misery of the factory system, which had disrupted the traditional pattern of economic activity, and as a means by which a growing and exploited working-class could defend itself against the hard, new masters, who demanded the maximum of effort in return for the least possible reward. Socialism grew to maturity as capitalist enterprise spread across the world, and the utopian schemes of the pioneers were discarded for a more elaborate indictment of the capitalist society, which seemed unable to prevent recurrent wars and financial crises. The second half of the nineteenth century was the great period in which rival groups thrashed out the main theoretical problems of socialism and laid the foundations of the mass movements we know today. In the last thirty years socialists have spent part of their time refining and extending doctrines whose basic principles were clearly established before 1914, and, for the rest, meeting the tactical difficulties that arose from their increasing strength and from the prospect, in a number of countries, that they would be called upon to accept the responsibilities of power.

But socialism, like other philosophies, owes a great deal to the past. Though, as a serious movement of social criticism and reform, it dates back barely a hundred and fifty years, its ancestry can be traced to some of the greatest figures in the cultural and political life of Europe. It is one aspect of the civilised tradition that started in ancient Greece and Rome. It has inherited the radical interpretation of Christianity. Continental socialism, in part, sprang from the philosophy of Hegel. Under quite different conditions, the utilitarian Jeremy Bentham left an abiding mark on the English labour movement which grew up after his death in 1832. Rousseau, too, Tom Paine and others who led the democratic assault on privilege and autocracy, are now acclaimed as men who marked out the road that socialism was later to follow.

There is nothing new in the idea that misery and injustice are the result of the division of society into rich and poor. In European literature, up to the dawn of the machine era, there was a recurring belief in a lost golden age when, before the advent of civilisation with its attendant vices of poverty and privilege, men lived a simple pastoral life, holding all things in common. Socialism, at least as much as any other contemporary doctrine, is the heir to that intermingling of Greek philosophy, Roman law and Christian religion on which the democratic tradition rests. In early socialist speculation there are frequent appeals to antiquity. Mably, the French philosopher of the eighteenth century, who provided most of the intellectual inspiration for the abortive communist revolt led by Babeuf in the last stages of the French Revolution, drew heavily upon Plato and Lycurgus of Sparta. The Christian teachings, even the communal life of the early Christians themselves, powerfully influenced the peasant revolts at the close of the Middle Ages, the extreme Left-wing groups in the English Civil War, and, more recently, some of the chief founders of the Labour Party in Britain.

Socialism today is not only a vision of what life could be like in rational society; it is also a political technique. Most socialists regard the working-class as the social group which presses most consistently for the limitation of the abuses of capitalism and its eventual overthrow. To accomplish this task, organisation is necessary. Socialist parties work within the framework of the capitalist State to secure, either by reform or revolution, the political power they require to shape both the institutions and economic structure of society to their ends.

Before the rise of modern industry, with its immense productive capacities, and the emergence of an organised working-class seeking to transfer the ownership and control of production from private to public hands, socialism, as we know it, was an impossibility. There were many critics in the past who showed a penetrating insight into the causes of distress, injustice and discontent. Some of them went futher and envisaged the broad outlines of a more harmonious and prosperous world. But the resources, the technical development and political methods of achieving it were lacking, and they had to fall back on remedies which were doomed from the start to failure.

All the same, their work was not fruitless. They kept the socialist tradition alive until the day when it became something more than a vision. They desired fraternity and equality among men; they insisted that the unequal distribution of wealth and power was the origin of misery and corruption; and they dreamed of a regenerated society where men, no longer divided into masters and servants, would co-operate for the common good.

By general consent the most remarkable of these pioneers was Sir Thomas More. His *Utopia*, published in 1516, is the greatest of all social fantasies. Unlike many similar works, it was not constructed out of abstract ideas, nor does it glance back to a happy pastoral society lost in the shadows of history. More was one of the foremost statesmen of his age, a man of great personal integrity and intellectual ability. Much of his *Utopia* is devoted to a description of England at the beginning of the sixteenth century, when the breakdown of the static medieval economy was raising new and unprecedented problems. Great fortunes were being made in commerce, especially in the developing wool trade, while the peasantry were being driven from the land and their places taken by the more profitable sheep. Through the mouth of a Portuguese explorer, Raphael Hythloday, More tells the story of the island of Utopia as a contrast to the state of England, where private property, the exclusion of the many from the means of life for the benefit of the few, is the root of evil. 'Where possessions are private, where money is the measure of all things,' says Hythloday, 'it is hard and almost impossible that the common-wealth should have just government and enjoy prosperity.'

But in Utopia, where the citizens pool the products of their labour and draw what they need from the common storehouse, there is peace and security. Men under communism have neither need nor desire for personal wealth to ensure their comfort and freedom from oppression. The people of Utopia, unlike the unhappy English, understand that the scramble for riches is the root of ambition, of civil strife, of wars, even of the decay of nations. *Utopia* is probably the finest work produced by any of the primitive communist writers. Unlike most of them, More saw that a workable communist system must control production as well as ensure an equal distribution of goods. Though he shared their inability to suggest any really practical way of accomplishing the transition of the ideal community, none of them rivalled him in scope or clarity of description. His *Utopia* has survived, to our own time, as a brilliant picture of the life that men both could and ought to live.

For more than a hundred years before the publication of More's remarkable book there had been an undercurrent of discontent among the English peasantry, which at times broke out into open revolt. Heresy, encouraged by itinerant friars, was widespread. The peasants, increasingly divorced from the land, lacking any social rights, sought the restitution of ancient Christian equality and the abolition of the pomp and splendour of contemporary Catholicism. It was but a short step for them to demand the elimination of civil privilege and the sharing of all property. In the Peasant Revolt of 1381, the priest, John Ball, preached the brotherhood of men, created equal by nature and deprived of their rights by lords, judges and lawyers.

On the Continent, like heresies led to peasant wars. Mystical sects, such as the Bohemian Taborites and Münzer in Germany, managed to dominate large districts for years. Even after their violent suppression their ideas lingered on in Europe. In those days, it must be remembered, all thought was cast in the religious mould of the Catholic Church. Social discontent could only become articulate as a heresy, which was then bitterly attacked by the combined efforts of the princes and the Church. Yet, in spite of brutality and bloodshed, these plebeian heresies flourished among the peasants and among the poorer townsmen, keeping alive the early Christian doctrine that private property was sinful and an obstacle to salvation. The communitarian ideas of the Anabaptists and others continued to exert an influence down to modern times—Leo Tolstoy's ideas owed much to this tradition.

By the beginning of the English Civil War, in 1642, Puritanism, which had begun as a heresy, had taken hold among the wealthy commercial class in the towns. It was a democratic doctrine, developed in the struggle against an obsolete monarchy and a corrupt Church. Throughout this revolutionary period it served as a suitable ideology for a merchant capitalism which was successfully destroying the political, economic and religious fetters that handicapped the expansion of trade, the easy and profitable circulation of capital and the establishment of a representative, if at that time limited, democracy. But in times of social upheaval more radical ideas are always brought to the fore. By 1648 the rank-and-file of the Parliamentary armies had swung over to support the Levellers, who sought to carry the new democratic ideas to their logical conclusion, to attack all privilege, and to claim the earth as the natural inheritance of all men. The Levellers concentrated upon political reform: there is an implicit socialism in their doctrine, but it is never stated. Still couching their philosophy in religious language, they found their golden age in Saxon England, before the Norman Conquest had placed a privileged and alien hierarchy in power and driven its rightful owners from their communal enjoyment of the soil of England.

This idea was expressed even more forcibly by Gerard Winstanley, the leader of a small group known as the Diggers. Unlike the Levellers, they had little faith in political action of the normal kind and they were much more precise about the society they wished to set up immediately in England. Declaring that the Civil War had been fought to restore their rights to the people of England, in April 1649 Winstanley and some of his followers began to dig the common at St. George's Hill, Weybridge. They were later driven off by a troop of cavalry. Winstanley then turned writer and worked out a doctrine to justify his action. In some remarkable passages he anticipates much that figures prominently in later socialism. Society, he said, is divided into warring classes. Political struggles are a reflection of property interests. Co-operative work and collective possession must one day replace hired labour and private ownership if men are to enjoy freedom, happiness and prosperity.

Winstanley's experiment failed, inevitably. Though, for another two hundred years, no one in England produced a more brilliant or realistic socialist analysis, he had little influence upon his own or subsequent generations. Yet, indirectly, he is linked to the modern socialist movement. Some of his ideas were embodied in a book, written by John Bellers in 1696, called *The College of Industry*, which advocated a system of co-operative and self-supporting communities. Many years afterwards a copy of this book fell into the hands of Robert Owen, the factory owner, who is generally regarded as the father of the early nineteenth-century socialist and co-operative moments in Britain. In acknowledging his debt to Bellers, as he did, Owen was also paying a tribute to Winstanley.

There are important similarities between the Civil War in England and the French Revolution. In the same way the struggle against feudalism was at first undertaken by the moderate middle-class parties, which, under the strain of war and social dislocation, were increasingly challenged by more extreme groups, composed partly of the poor and propertyless. But these events in France took place more than a hundred years later and were influenced by the political thought and experience of those intervening years.

In England, at the end of the revolutionary upheaval, there appeared the mystic agrarian reformer Winstanley. In France the final stages of the Revolution threw up Babeuf and his militant communist conspiracy.

Before Babeuf, who stands at the divide between primitive and modern socialism, there are a few French writers who can justly be associated with the socialist tradition. Two of them, Mably and Morelly, both widely read in their own day, were advocates of a full, if fantastic, communism, and they undoubtedly had a considerable influence upon Babeuf. Rousseau, the most influential of all the French philosophers, certainly cannot be called a socialist. But his passionate attacks on wealth, his denunciations of the corrupting environment of society, his eulogy of equality and his insistence that primitive men had once held all things in common, left their mark on Jacobins like Marat and Robespierre, and on groups that stood even further to the Left.

After the fall of Robespierre it was clear that the individualist peasant and the speculator had profited most from the sacrifices of the Revolution. Babeuf, and the other remarkable men associated with him in the 'Conspiracy of the Equals', sought to carry the struggle a stage further. Whereas most primitive socialists had contented themselves with charting the details of a new society—and Babeuf himself worked out the main features of his communist State with some care—they had failed to evolve a practicable means of winning and maintaining power to accomplish the transition. Babeuf, for the first time, produced a revolutionary technique. He did this with such skill that the methods of the conspirators have provided the basis of revolutionary socialist strategy ever since. They appealed directly to the Parisian working-class; they developed an elaborate propaganda machine; they formed secret cells in the army and the police. Since the rich will never voluntarily surrender their power, they said, it must be taken from them by force.

After the success of the revolt, a dictatorship is necessary for the period of transition to communist democracy, but work will be provided for all, there will be free medical services and education, the prison system will be reformed and the aged will receive State pensions. The individual will fulfil himself in the service of the whole community. Private property will be abolished, since it is an incitement to civil war and prevents men sharing equally in wealth and happiness.

There is much in the outlook of the conspirators that reveals how far they were truly forerunners of modern socialist thought. Their revolt failed and Babeuf himself died on the guillotine. But they left an enduring legacy. One of them, Buonarroti, later wrote the history of the conspiracy, after spending thirty years working with men who played a leading part in the foundation of socialist groups in France, Britain, Belgium and Germany. Babeuf brought something new to socialism. He, more than anyone else, stands at the beginning of the road that led to Lenin and the Bolshevik Revolution of 1917. He was the first socialist of any importance to declare that working-class power could be won by a revolution as carefully prepared as a military operation.

Though the Napoleonic Empire placed the rich and the privileged in power again, it did not restore the old régime. France was no longer a feudal country. The speculator had replaced the aristocratic landlord; the serf had been turned into a free peasant. Capitalist social relationships were spreading fast. Yet the intense political experience of the Revolution could not easily be forgotten. Socialist ideas were no longer an abstract doctrine. Men had learnt that the State might be used to abolish privilege, to direct production and control distribution, to give reward according to need, to sustain the interests of the poor against the greed and exploitation of the rich.

France, at this time, seemed to have lost its sense of political direction. The old régime had vanished: the new age of industry and commerce was scarcely born. Henri de Saint-Simon believed that he had an answer. Of aristocratic origins, he had fought in the American War of Independence and had seen for himself the birth of a new democratic republic, based on the hard work of merchants and farmers. Where, he asked, were men to find the sources of political and spiritual power which could replace all that had been lost with the overthrow of feudalism? They should embrace a new religion that would replace the orthodox Christianity, which had completed its historic mission. They should behave as brothers, they should subordinate everything to the effort 'to ameliorate as promptly and as quickly as possible the moral and physical existence of the most numerous class'.

This idea that the proper function of the State is to ensure the welfare of the masses was Saint-Simon's greatest contribution to political thought, though he himself was no socialist in the modern sense. He believed in the retention of privilege and private property, as long as both status and wealth were the reward of hard work of value to the community. He thought all men should be given equal opportunities in life, but he was willing to concede the capitalist his profits if he understood that property also entailed social responsibilities. There is much, in fact, in his philosophy which can be interpreted as an intelligent anticipation of the practices of private enterprise in an industrial society, even of the corporate State. But, on the other hand, by a slight change in emphasis, part of his doctrine was easily turned into a socialist critique of capitalism.

Later in the nineteenth century Marxism was to take from him the thesis that one day political government would be replaced by the expert administration of production and distribution, though, for Marx and Engels, that day would come only when the victory of full communism had eliminated the need for the State as an instrument of class rule. Saint-Simon, moreover, was the first social philosopher to relate the growth of science and the technical revolution which proceeded from it to form a theory of historical development which could explain, coherently, the course of man and society through the ages. In this, too, he can be said to anticipate Marx and Engels.

Besides Saint-Simon there was another eccentric Frenchman who is now regarded as one of the socialist pioneers. Charles Fourier was also far from being a consistent or coherent socialist. He had a passion for completing his pictures of social organization down to the last comma. Though his imagination often ran riot in the universe as well as on this planet, to a degree which is both baffling and amusing, he had a considerable influence for many years after his death in 1837. Commerce, he said, made virtue less lucrative than vice. Every individual is at war with the interests of the community in his search for personal wealth. This unnecessary competition produces only waste and parasitism—a conclusion that evoked a wide response in France. If work is to be made pleasant and attractive, if men are to be happy, they must establish co-operative settlements—to which he gave the name of phalanxes—in which there would be an opportunity for everyone to find employment which would be both lucrative and suitable for the creative expression of personality. Fourier did not desire a barrack-room equality within his phalanx. On the contrary, wealth would be no sin provided it was achieved by co-operative means. But every individual would be guaranteed a minimum standard of life.

Fourier, typically, worked out the last administrative and constructional details of his phalanxes. Stripped of its obvious absurdities, his idea was sufficiently attractive to inspire a number of experiments. But the fate of the colonies founded on Fourier's model in both Europe and America was a demonstration of the futility of trying to change the structure of society by example. In the early nineteenth century success went to the men who were transforming the face of the world by the development of industry and commerce, not to those who spent their energies in the formation of idyllic self-supporting communities.

The followers of Saint-Simon did not waste their strength in the fashion of many energetic Fourierists. In spite of internal quarrels and the difficulties into which the Saint-Simonian school fell when its more extreme members tried to carry out the moral and religious precepts of their master, it produced a flood of propaganda aimed, with some accuracy, at the abuses consequent upon the development of industrial capitalism. It attacked inheritance and denounced exploitation; it insisted that the State should eventually own the land and the factories, and direct production in the interests of the community as a whole. Its teachings, in a simplified form, became associated with the discontent among the growing working-class of France. Its enthusiasm for vast public works found an echo in later French socialism. Some of the Saint-Simonians, who were a brilliant group of young men, afterwards became prominent business men and engineers who were largely responsible, among other achievements, for the building of the French railway system and the Suez Canal.

But by 1830 new forces were at work. The 'utopian socialists', as they were later and firmly classified by Marx and Engels in the *Communist Manifesto*, had laid the groundwork for their successors in the age of industry and had little more to say or do. In their day they were men of remarkable, though erratic, insight. They arose in a period of transition. They never had to face the problems of a highly-organised industrial system.

The modern working-class movement had not then developed, and they had no real idea of how a new social order could be set up. They appealed to humanity as a whole to be guided by their rational doctrine and, lacking any adequate sense of the pattern of historical development, did not understand that a ruling class does not voluntarily relinquish its power. They believed that it was only necessary for a man of genius to appear and proclaim the need for a new and regenerated society for all men to realise that their prosperity and happiness depended on the acceptance of his doctrine. Yet, for all their weaknesses, these men were the pioneers of modern socialism. Most of them devoted their lives to the struggle to free their fellow men from want, misery and oppression. It is remarkable how much of modern socialism—especially of its moral criticism—was anticipated in their writings. Marx himself, though critical of their shortcomings, was heavily in their debt; and in recent years, when 'revisionist' Marxists reacted against the totalitarian aspects of Soviet Communism, there has been a new interest in the humanist tradition exemplified by their early socialists. For them, the ideal of human fraternity was as important as any theory of social change or any system of political tactics—and it is this idealism which stamps all their work.

3

OWEN AND THE CHARTISTS

In the first half of the nineteenth century the foundations of modern industry and socialism were firmly laid in Great Britain. On the Continent the working-class emerged as an important and independent political force only during the revolutions in 1848. But by that time the British proletariat had already created its own mass party and trade union organisations, experimented with co-operative enterprises, and, from a variety of teachers, learnt the essentials of socialism. While Britain was leading the world in the development of the industrial capitalist system, the workers were trying out in an embryonic form many of the methods and ideas which later were embodied in classical socialist theory.

There were propertyless wage-earners, with trade clubs to defend their interests, for a long time before the discovery of steam power and the other mechanical inventions which revolutionised industrial technique. But, in the absence of the factory system on a national scale, the strikes and protests of these workers were limited to particular areas or specific grievances; they could not possess either a sense of common purpose or the capacity for large-scale organisation in their own interest.

Nevertheless, in the bigger towns in the woollen and mining industries a growing number of artisans and workers were caught up in the democratic agitation for the reform of the corrupt Parliamentary system. The London masses were brought into action by the struggle between their champion, John Wilkes, and the House of

Commons, which refused to seat him. But until after the end of the Napoleonic Wars the initiative was taken by the skilled craftsmen, rather than by the misery-ridden miners and operatives.

It was the artisans who had formed the London Corresponding Society and similar groups in Manchester, Sheffield and other towns. These were the first definitely political bodies of working-men. They were content, on the whole, to act under the leadership of the middle-class reform movement, but before long they also became the spokesmen of the larger and less articulate class of workers which lacked either their education or their income.

The French Revolution was a great stimulant to the democrats in Britain. Its ideas were spread throughout the country by Tom Paine, Thomas Hardy and other agitators. Demands for universal suffrage, for annual Parliaments, even for a republic, increased rapidly. But the movement was crushed before it achieved anything substantial. The network of corresponding societies was broken up by a series of treason trials after 1793. Many of the middle-class reformers were terrified into desertion by Pitt's campaign of repression and by the ruthlessness of Jacobin policy in France. Later, the naval mutinies at the Nore and Spithead, and the rebellion of the United Irishmen, provided a further scare for the middle-classes.

It was not merely political activity that was suppressed. The Combination Acts of 1799 and 1800 made all trade combinations illegal, though these laws were applied with a severity that varied from year to year and from one place to another, according to the strength of working-class discontent. But, under the pressure of war, industry was growing rapidly and trade unionism carried on an underground struggle among the workers, whose numbers increased every year.

The end of the Napoleonic Wars marked the start of a new phase in the reform movement. The workers, faced with widespread unemployment, again rallied behind the middle-class demand for a radical change in the British Constitution. The oligarchic Government of the time, in spite of new legislation and persecution—such as the Six Acts and the infamous massacre at St. Peter's Fields ('Peterloo') in 1819—found that the business men and industrialists were not prepared to join in the suppression of working-class organisations which supported their campaign. The French menace was over, and the middle-classes were no longer satisfied to be ruled by an oligarchy which refused to admit them to their proper share of political power and restricted the growth of commerce and industry.

The face of Britain was changing fast. Between 1770 and 1820 more than five million acres of the common land had been expropriated by the richer landowners by the Enclosure Acts. The peasantry, driven from the soil, moved into the new towns like Manchester, where they could find work in the factories and mills. Men, women and children worked more than fourteen hours a day for little more than a bare subsistence wage and slept at nights in filthy hovels which were the breeding-ground of cholera and other diseases. They lived and died like animals and their masters grew wealthy on their misery. Naturally, many of them struck out blindly in self-defence. The ruined handloom-weavers tried to smash the new machines that they believed had caused their misery. But these sporadic revolts were always crushed.

Masses of the workers took part in the agitation which at last secured the Reform Act of 1832 and thereby served their political apprenticeship. The Combination Acts were repealed in 1824 and trade unions were once more able to operate openly. For the time, however, political rather than industrial action seemed the best means of securing a general improvement in the conditions of the working-class. As the Tory wing of the oligarchy could not be overthrown by violence, the Whigs, as the only other effective group in Parliament, had to carry through the long-overdue reforms. Under pressure from the commercial and industrial class—for whose democratic views they had almost as much distaste as the Tories—they were at last induced to grant a limited franchise to the middle-class, though this was done only in the belief that it would be of assistance in the traditional contest with the Tory section of the aristocracy.

The workers, who had been the mainstay of the agitation in the country, got nothing for their efforts. The radical reformers had encouraged them to believe that a thorough house-cleaning at Westminster would open the road to their emancipation, but there was never any intention of fulfilling the demagogic promises made to the starving illiterate and desperate masses at the height of the struggle. Angry and disillusioned, and by now experienced in politics, the workers formed their own organisations to take up the fight again.

It was in the Chartist period that followed that socialism became an important political force. But the ground had already been prepared. There were a number of radical writers who influenced the leaders of the growing working-class. Some, like Charles Hall, John Bray, William Thompson, Thomas Hodgskin and John Gray showed a remarkable insight into the character of the new industrial society. They condemned the great maldistribution of wealth and the inquities of privilege. The mass of the people, they said, was doomed to a life of ignorance, poverty and ill-health. In his brilliant *Lecture on Human Happiness* John Gray developed the idea that exploitation was inherent in the capitalist system, a thesis also advanced by Thompson in his *Distribution of Wealth*, which denounced the capitalist for denying the labourer the reward of his work. Hodgskin, though he was more of an individualist, anticipated the Marxist belief that human history is moulded by economic factors, and argued that the workers would come into their own only after the abolition of class divisions and of government as the instrument by which the rich maintained their rights of property.

The most significant contribution of this group, however, was the use it made of the economics of David Ricardo, the stockbroker, as a foundation of socialist theory. The doctrine that labour is the only source of value and has a right to the whole reward of its efforts was the logical conclusion of Ricardo's argument. It underlay the work of almost every socialist up to and including Marx, who placed it at the centre of his economic analysis.

None of these men, however, can be credited with achievements equal to those of Robert Owen. Born in 1771, apprenticed to a draper at the age of ten, he was the manager of a large mill by the time he was twenty. He was one of the most able industrialists of his time, and soon acquired a considerable fortune. But he was, fortunately, not typical of this class. He held unorthodox views on religion— which were later to be a serious embarrassment to him—and on the importance of environment as a determinant of character. He, practically alone in the early nineteenth century, insisted that decent

B

education, wages and working conditions were essential for the proper development of human personality, and proved by his own example that they were not the road to ruin for manufacturers, as so many believed. In the years of depression after the Napoleonic Wars he began to urge the establishment of co-operative communities along the lines of his remarkable factory at New Lanark. He received some support from the Government to begin with—the Tory Prime Minister, Lord Sidmouth, sent copies of Owen's *New View of Society* to a number of European rulers for their comments—but he was soon attacked both by the ruling class and some of the reformers, one regarding him as a dangerous revolutionary and the other as a reactionary philanthropist.

Owen, in his personal attitude, was certainly a benevolent autocrat, but his teachings soon found a response among the workers. He understood that men could make the most effective use of the vast productive powers of industry if they co-operated for the common good, eliminated private ownership and profit, and set up self-governing industrial and agricultural communities. To prove his point he spent his fortune in a series of futile attempts to establish such colonies in Britain and in the New World. He returned to England in 1829, after spending four years in the United States, to find that the workers had taken up his ideas.

Artisans and factory operatives alike saw in the co-operative community a means by which they could free themselves from the exploitation of the employers, could escape into decent living conditions away from the squalor of the new towns, and, while retaining the valuable features of industry, could regain contact with the land from which they had been driven. A large part of the working-class, after the treachery of the reformers in 1832, was willing to accept a gospel which showed it how direct industrial, rather than political, action could lead it to a democratic and prosperous society.

By 1833 Owen's ideas had a firm hold in the trade unions that were springing up all over the country, and had inspired a number of producer and consumer co-operative enterprises. John Doherty, one of the outstanding union leaders, was a strong Owenite, and he was associated with Owen in fighting for factory reform and the eight-hour day in the North of England. Owen himself managed to establish the Grand National Consolidated Trades Union, which, at its height, claimed over half a million members.

The unions which composed this body did not confine themselves to agitation on wages and hours. They attempted to set up workshops which would compete with those of their masters and eventually drive them out of business. Rejecting political action in the electoral sense, for a time they favoured the idea of a general strike as a means of transition to the new society of co-operation and equality. But, for all its hopes, the movement crumbled as fast as it was built, its strength wasted in a series of exhausting strikes and lock-outs.

The savage sentence passed upon the Tolpuddle landworkers in 1834 for their attempt to form a branch of Owen's union was answered by protest meetings throughout Britain, but the prosecution accelerated the disintegration of the Grand National Consolidated Trades Union. In little less than a year after its foundation it was wound up and the active leadership of the working-class passed from Owen into other hands.

Owen himself lived on for another twenty years, but his work was done. He had produced a coherent philosophy—even the word 'socialism' was first used in an Owenite paper—and built a great though short-lived movement. Finally, it was his ideas that inspired the Rochdale Equitable Pioneers to start the modern movement of consumers' co-operation in 1844.

Almost immediately after the collapse of the Owenite movement, and while Owen's doctrine still found widespread support, the British working-class again took up the struggle for the political rights which they had failed to win in the agitation for the Reform Act. For the next ten years, while the men of property trembled at the prospect of revolution, the demand for the People's Charter was pressed forward by vast demonstrations, petitions, riots, and even sporadic attempts at rebellion. Chartism—and this was one of the reasons for its ultimate failure—was not a homogeneous movement. To some of its supporters the platform of universal suffrage, annual parliaments and payment for members was sufficient for an immediate end. Others, however, regarded it as merely the first step along the road to a socialist republic. Both revolutionaries and reformists agreed that political power should be secured by the working-class.

But there was no common opinion about the way that power should be won or about the use that should be made of it after victory.

William Lovett and his associates in the London Working Men's Association, who first drew up the Charter in 1837, were skilled artisans who believed in patient and rational propaganda for reform. They had no intention of leading a mass movement which often threatened to turn into a national insurrection, and were quite prepared to work with the radical elements of the middle-class within and without Parliament to carry the Charter.

But events moved too rapidly for them. Following the passage of the Poor Law Amendment Act in 1834, at a time when the conditions of life for the factory operatives and landworkers were literally murderous, the old system of subsidising wages from the rates was abolished, and the poor driven into workhouses, where deliberate starvation and cruelty were the rule. The Poor Law agitation in the industrial North could not be halted by repression. It quickly came under the leadership of the Chartists, who were the only group capable of giving it coherence and organisation. The struggle for the Charter, by peaceful or violent means, seemed the only hope for men ground down by the joint despotism of capitalism and the ruling oligarchy.

Chartism failed, though it at one time had a majority behind it. There was no chance of arresting capitalist development in Britain at that stage or of an immature working-class movement winning its battle with the new alliance of landlords and industrialists. Nevertheless, the Chartist movement was the first mass proleterian organisation to attempt this task. It was a school in which socialist theory and tactics were taught, not only to the British workers but to the European workers as well.

Though it declined rapidly at the end of the 'forties, it had a lasting influence in the nineteenth century. It was divided, as all socialist movements have since been split, between reformists with a devotion to constitutional procedure and a revolutionary wing which believed that the working-class could only triumph by a violent assault upon a State which they saw as an instrument of capitalist domination. The two groups fought for the leadership of the movement, and each blamed its failure on the follies of the other.

Neither, at that time, could have secured the desired success. In its absence the British workers turned to other methods, to support the cheap bread agitation of the Anti-Corn Law League, to consumers' co-operation, to the construction of non-socialist trade unionism and, on the whole, a policy of sharing to a small extent in the wealth which capitalism was bringing to Britain from every corner of the world.

Yet this short survey of Chartism would not be complete without some mention of men such as George Julian Harney and Bronterre O'Brien. Both of them were extreme socialists and both were strongly influenced by the French Revolution.

In articles—chiefly in the *Poor Man's Guardian* and the Chartist *Northern Star*—in pamphlets and speeches, Harney and O'Brien continually took a wider view of the struggle than most of their contemporaries, and attempted to thrash out a working-class philosophy which would both explain and justify what they were trying to do. O'Brien translated Buonarotti's history of Babeuf's communist conspiracy. Though, later in life, he became lost in a confusion of his own economic ideas, in the Chartist period he was far ahead of most of his fellow propagandists in his perception that working-class misery was due to the structure of capitalist industry rather than to the personal villainy of the employers. He had a clear understanding of the nature and importance of the class struggle.

Unlike many of the Chartists, including their most prominent leader, the fiery demagogue Feargus O'Connor, he did not wish to substitute peasant smallholdings for the tyranny of the machine, but realised that industry could be made the servant instead of the master of the worker. He attacked both Church and State as means by which property held the people in subjection. He fought the idea of Owen and the other utopian socialists that society could be converted by example and that the capture of political power was unimportant. In short, he had moved a long way towards the theories that Marx and Engels were to weave together in the doctrine of historical materialism. Harney, unlike O'Brien, was a young man at the peak of the Chartist movement: though he was one of the most powerful supporters of revolutionary methods for carrying the Charter, he never rivalled the theoretical brilliance of O'Brien, and his importance is due more to the way he maintained the socialist tradition after Chartism disintegrated—in spite of his instability and his political egotism—than to his merits as a thinker. In many respects Marxism stands in the direct line of descent from Chartism. Together with Ernest Jones, another of the younger Chartists, Harney represents the link between the two.

Chartism was not socialism, but it provided the experience upon which socialism and the working-class movement could be built. Before the further development of industry raised new problems and also fresh possibilities for the workers, they had experimented with constitutionalism, with the general strike, and with insurrection, all three methods upon which modern movements have relied. They had come to realise that the wheels of progress could not be reversed and the lost glories of peasant farming restored. Capitalism, it was clear, had come to stay, and they had to make terms with it. Though the revolutionary tradition never died out, the mass of the British working-class was ready to improve its conditions of life within the existing system. It was not willing to waste its strength in futile efforts to overthrow it. After the fiasco of the last major Chartist demonstration in April 1848, at a time when the European proletariat was on the barricades, the marriage between socialism and the working-class movement was temporarily dissolved in Britain. The elaboration of socialist doctrine went on steadily, but it had comparatively little influence on the men who were building up their new trade union and co-operative organisations.

4

FRANCE AND GERMANY

The Powers which defeated Napoleonic France met in the Congress of Vienna in 1815. They tried to make a settlement which would not only lessen the danger of recurrent war, but also check the social unrest and agitation that was spreading throughout Europe. In the first task they were successful for four decades; in the second they were defeated by the alliance of liberalism and nationalism, and by the fact that the growth of capitalist industry released new political and economic forces which steadily undermined the European structure built and maintained by Metternich as a bulwark against reform.

The working-class developed later and more spasmodically in Europe than in Britain. In the years before 1848 it was only important in a few centres—Paris, for instance—where it worked politically as the Left wing of the democratic and republican movement. In some countries the awakening of national consciousness distracted attention from social issues and united the people against foreign despotism. Until the national question was settled in lands like Italy, Poland and, to a lesser extent, Germany, there was little chance of any significant socialist thought or organisation making much headway. The peasantry, up to at least the middle of the nineteenth century, was the predominant group in all European States, and on the whole it was deeply religious, hostile to the towns, and a prop for any strong government.

The history of these years is the struggle between the ideas launched on the world by the French Revolution and the old autocratic and backward monarchies which still sought to arrest the development of liberty, democracy and industry. In almost every country of Europe this issue was fought out. In some the revolutionaries sought to liberate their nation; in others the liberals demanded a constitution. Everywhere the conservatives found themselves on the defensive. Their police were continually unearthing conspiracies organised by the secret societies in which the revolutionaries were forced by persecution to organise. There certainly was not any central organisation directing the activities of the liberals in every nation, but, in the words of the chief of the Paris police in 1825, 'they had one language, one code of morality, one religion, a common political aim'. It was in these conditions that socialism emerged in France and Germany.

In July 1830 Charles X was overthrown by a revolution in Paris. The Bourbon monarchy, reimposed on France by the victorious Powers in 1815, which represented the wealthy landowners and such of the old aristocracy as had survived the guillotine, was replaced by a new régime. Charles was succeeded by Louis Philippe, Duke of Orleans, who was sponsored by the financiers and speculators who had enriched themselves at the expense of the State and the peasantry.

It was not long before the radicals and republicans realised that they had manned the barricades only to bring the bankers to power. The secret societies again became active. There was an abortive insurrection in 1832 in Paris, and another at Lyons in 1834. In 1839 conspirators belonging to the Society of the Seasons seized the Paris Town Hall before their revolt was crushed. The leader of the society was Auguste Blanqui, an extraordinary man who spent a great deal of his life serving a series of prison sentences and the remainder in organising the revolutionary workpeople of Paris.

Blanqui was essentially a pupil of Gracchus Babeuf. He had learnt at first-hand the political ideas and methods of the Conspiracy of the Equals from Philippe Buonarroti, its historian, with whom he had been associated in the Parisian secret societies, and tried to apply them with little modification to the France of his time. Blanqui, however, was more realistic than most of his contemporary socialists in France and Germany. He, unlike the utopians, based his revolutionary tactics upon the class struggle of the workers against the capitalists and landlords who exploited and dictated to them. He was not much concerned with working out a detailed analysis of society or of the proletarian republic he wished to establish. On the other hand, he underestimated both the importance of the liberal effort to secure political democracy and of mass working-class organisation. Blanqui placed his faith in a *coup* accomplished by a small disciplined group of professional conspirators as a surprise assault, without any preliminary attempt to educate or prepare a large number of workers to support it.

Throughout his life—and he lived to see the Paris Commune of 1871—Blanqui never shook off the traditional methods of the secret society. As a result, in spite of his personal heroism and the services he rendered to French socialism in the days when both it and he were young, he could not understand or participate in the new movements which grew up after the revolutionary upheavals of 1848. He, and those whom he inspired and led, remained an influential group in French socialism until after the suppression of the Paris Commune. In 1917 Lenin—despite his criticisms of Blanqui—was to adopt his technique and make a successful rising in Petrograd: the Babouvist tradition at last came into its own.

Neither Blanqui's ideas nor his methods could provide an adequate philosophy for the majority of the French workers. For this they turned elsewhere, above all to Louis Blanc and to Pierre-Joseph Proudhon. These two men differed widely in personality and outlook, but between them they provided most of the intellectual inspiration of the mass socialist movement.

Louis Blanc was the first socialist of any importance to believe that the State could be used as an instrument of reform rather than as a machine for the domination of one class by another. He could not accept Blanqui's argument that liberal reforms were mere hypocrisy and that the working-class could achieve its salvation only by an insurrection which would be followed by a dictatorship directed against the rich. He supported the agitation for universal suffrage on the grounds that a democratically elected government could first alleviate the misery of the people and then, gradually, replace competitive capitalism by co-operative factories and services. In 1839, at the age of twenty-eight, he published his best book, *The Organisation of Work*. In it he suggested that the State should set up social workshops, supplying capital and machinery for the purpose. The mines, banks and railways, taken over by the State, would provide its revenue. The workers would learn the art of management; their right to employment would be guaranteed; and the capitalists he so brilliantly indicted would be given the option of joining the system of workshops or being driven out of business by their superior efficiency.

Blanc, to use a modern phrase, was a reformist. He was more concerned with working out practical schemes upon which France could immediately be set to work than with agitating the Paris masses to revolt in the name of millenial socialist doctrines. His insistence upon the right to work and his plan for national workshops, it is true, stirred many of those who fought in the 1848 insurrections, but he was in many ways the forerunner of later gradualist socialism, with its belief that, in time, it would attain power by electoral methods and proceed, by steady if slow steps, to use the existing State as a means of securing both economic stability and the better welfare of its working-class.

During 1848, when Blanc himself was a junior member of the revolutionary government, national workshops were actually set up to absorb some of the unemployed. Though they retained the name which Blanc had popularised, they were intended by his non-socialist colleagues in the Provisional Government to be a failure. They were tried only to damp down working-class agitation and to discredit Blanc himself by their futility. From 1852 until 1879 Blanc was an exile in London. He returned to France and, in spite of his claim that he was still a socialist, opposed the proletarian and revolutionary Paris Commune.

Proudhon was a very different type of man. He was neither successful nor realistic. His thought suffered from a lack of intellectual discipline. He was capable of brilliant criticism of other doctrines and parties, but he was unable to bind his own ideas with consistency or to purge them of serious confusions. He was self-educated and, though he had read very widely, never properly digested his material. In spite of his lasting influence on French socialism he never understood the character of the urban working-class, and until his death his outlook was dominated by the peasant background from which he sprang and the artisans among whom he lived. Nevertheless, he made a great impression in his day, and as recently as 1919 there was a Proudhonist revival in France as a reaction against the growing strength of Marxism.

Proudhon was essentially an individualist. He attacked the existing property relationships on the grounds that they frustrated the adequate development of human personality, which he believed was sacred above all else. The peasant is the individual at his best, for in an agricultural society a man fulfils himself in living by his own personal and direct efforts. Many of the earlier socialists, especially the primitives and utopians, had denounced the family as an obstacle to progress, but for Proudhon it is the only really good form of social organisation. Through the family, man learns to appreciate the moral virtues of justice, liberty, equality and chastity, the last of which is the greatest, for without it the family cannot survive. The possession of property is evil if it enables the owner to live without work, good if he uses it as a means to work. (In other words, landlords are as undesirable as peasant ownership is laudable.)

Proudhon not only disliked a State dominated by bankers; he condemned all States on principle. 'Government of man by man in every form is oppression,' he wrote, for 'the highest perfection of society is found in the union of order and anarchy.' Since the function of any State must be to protect property and privilege, it must be replaced by a federation of self-governing communes in which there would be neither rich nor poor, master nor servant.

Thus Proudhon's emphasis on the individual made him the protagonist of anarchism, of a society so free from the twin tyrannies of wealth and power that there would be no restrictions upon the liberty of the individual to fulfil himself as best he might. Proudhon's economic views were, if anything, as popular as his politics. In 1846 he published his *System of Economic Contradictions*, in which he argued that the social character of a society is determined more by the manner in which wealth circulates than by the methods by which it is produced. Therefore changes should be accomplished by alterations in the credit system. To this end he called for the establishment of credit banks which would lend money without interest and act as the centre of producers' co-operation. This idea swept through the workers in Paris and a few other towns.

At that time trade unions were prohibited in France, and in addition, owing to the late development of French industry, most workers were employed in small workshops. Thrown back upon themselves, the workers naturally took up a doctrine which placed individualism above collective organisation, and seemed to offer them the chance of becoming masters in their own right. Proudhon was certainly not a socialist in the normal sense. In many ways his views are reactionary, for he was trying to stop the development of both the State and a modern economic system status than his doctrine justifies, his protest against the conditions in which the French working-class knew itself to be living and his imprisonment for making that protest made him a teacher and a martyr.

Up to the revolt of February 1848 the Paris workers were by no means a distinct and organised opposition to the régime of Louis Philippe, though large numbers of them were active supporters of one of the socialist groups—of Louis Blanc, of Proudhon, of Blanqui, of the utopian communist Cabet, who wished to found an idyllic colony in the New World, of even the Saint-Simonians and the Fourierists.

The 1848 Revolution was a united effort by the middle-class and the workers to remove the corrupt monarchy, the government which Karl Marx later described as 'nothing other than a joint stock company for the exploitation of French national wealth'. The middle-class, which wanted to curb the financiers and speculators, and to stabilise expenditure which threatened to ruin the developing industry and commerce of France, split in two groups after the revolt succeeded. The first, representing the industrialists, desired a constitutional monarchy and some extension of the franchise; the second, based on the small merchants and business men, was more radical and favoured a republic.

After three months of uneasy compromise the Right wing won and succeeded in provoking the workers into an abortive insurrection, which was ruthlessly crushed. In the June fighting the Paris workers emerged as an independent political force for the first time, while the radical section of the middle-class deserted the Jacobin tradition and sided with the counter-revolution. The workers did not revolt in the name of socialism, but in their desperate misery they turned for leadership to socialists of many kinds, who offered some chance of an improvement in their lot. Up to this turning-point in European history the working-class had not been clearly distinguished from the mass of 'citizens' with radical views. After June 1848 the road lay open for new kinds of socialist theory and organisation based unambiguously upon the proletariat and directed against the capitalists who had at last become the masters of France.

Events in Germany followed a different course. The country was divided into a multitude of petty principalities. Though Prussia dominated them increasingly until it finally accomplished the unification of the German States into a nation, this task took nearly three-quarters of the nineteenth century. In Germany the struggle for national unity went hand in hand with the liberal demand for constitutional rights, bitterly opposed by both the rulers and their attendant bureaucracies in the greater and lesser States.

The Rhineland, however, was more advanced than the rest of the country owing to its more developed commerce and industry, and owing to its occupation by the French, and was the strongest centre of the reform movement. After 1813, in the revolutionary war against Napoleon, some progress was made, though neither the land reform nor the grant of limited political rights to the people was particularly far-reaching or effective. In spite of sporadic activity, German liberalism was a weak and immature force. Owing to the social conditions in the country, it was born late and suffered from a feeling of timidity and inferiority. It never engaged in a head-on clash with the old society as had its counterparts in England and France. Disunited, backward, reactionary, Germany was not a fertile soil for revolutionary organisation. The most intelligent and far-seeing thinkers were compelled to confine themselves largely to intellectual speculation, for want of opportunity to do anything else, as the poet Heine so brilliantly said in this satirical epigram:

> The French and Russians rule the land,
> The English rule the sea;
> But we in the airy realm of dreams
> Hold sovereign mastery.

This Germany produced great philosophers, of whom two at least—Fichte and Hegel—are the masters of much in later socialist thought. Of these Hegel was by far the more important.

The Hegelian philosophy could be interpreted in two ways. On one side it was an extremely sophisticated defence of things as they were; on the other, in the hands of a group known as the Young Hegelians, it developed into a number of different socialist schools of which the most outstanding was Marxism. Hegel as a conservative passed out of history with his times; Hegel as a man who revolutionised European philosophy remains an active influence today. He established the doctrine that change occurs in any field only as a result of a struggle between conflicting forces; that truth was not a collection of dogmatic statements which men could painfully assemble and then learn by rote; and that neither history nor knowledge can stand still at a pinnacle of achievement. History, said Hegel, is a continuous process. Each and every society is but a landmark on the endless pilgrimage of humanity from lower to higher states of life. This evolutionary process conforms to definite laws of development which can be ascertained and which, once discovered, can be used to chart the general direction in which a society is moving.

These ideas had tremendous possibilities as a means of analysis, and the Young Hegelians quickly seized the opportunity thus offered. They made penetrating criticisms of politics, history, religion, morals and even aesthetics. But, for all their brilliance, none of them rivalled a young doctor of philosophy called Karl Marx, who, denied a lectureship at the University of Bonn by the reactionary authorities, had turned to liberal journalism.

Marx was born in Trèves in 1818, of a Jewish family which had been converted to Christianity. By the time he was twenty-six his experiences as editor of the liberal *Rheinische Zeitung* had already led him to make a thorough study of the work of French socialist writers. When, for his activity, he was forced to emigrate to Paris, he had already worked out the basis of the materialist socialist philosophy which has ever since borne his name. In Paris in 1844, he came to know Heine, Proudhon and a host of other radical and proletarian revolutionaries, among them the man who was to be his lifelong friend and colleague, Friedrich Engels, the son of a prosperous Rhineland manufacturer and, like Marx, a Young Hegelian. In a symposium published by Marx in 1844 he included an article by Engels which, taken together with the latter's book on the working-class in England—written at the age of twenty-four after he had made a study of the Chartist Movement and come to know many prominent Chartists—shows that Engels had travelled a road similar to Marx in developing Hegel's dialectical philosophy into a socialist analysis of capitalist society.

From that moment on they collaborated as thinkers and organisers alike. When Marx was forced to leave Paris through the intervention of the Prussian Government, he went to Brussels and, joined at times by Engels, remained there until the outbreak of the revolutions of 1848, studying economics and political thought. In this period he and Engels produced *The Holy Family*, a polemic against their fellow Young Hegelians, and *The German Ideology*, a similar work; Marx alone wrote *The Poverty of Philosophy*, an attack on Proudhon's doctrine.

Little attention was paid to these books by Leninists or Stalinists; it was only after Stalin's death that there was a revival of interest in them when it was found that they expressed a sophisticated theory of human alienation—in the manner in which society distorts human personality, and specifically the way in which capitalist society creates deep psychological conflicts for the individual. The similarity of Marx's views to many of those held by modern social psychology, and some schools of psychotherapy, awakened interest in these long-neglected aspects of his work; while many Marxist 'revisionists' found in these writings a means of retaining a belief in Marxism while rejecting the 'distortions' imposed on Marx by Lenin, Stalin and other communist ideologists.

These books contain a much more explicit statement of some parts of Marx's philosophy than he was ever to write again. By 1848, Marx had done the groundwork on which historical materialism rests. Later, he extended this to an analysis of the economic structure of society, embodied in his great work, *Capital*, and to practical problems of politics. Neither Marx nor Engels believed that it was possible to codify their views into a fixed and final system of thought. They continually insisted that they had worked out a *method* of analysing and tackling social and historical questions, not a philosophy which anyone could learn from a textbook. Their lives, as much as their books, are the sources to which the student of Marxism must turn. All the time they were actively organising the international working-class movement they were refining, extending and applying their basic theories to the changing state of European society. Marxism, true to its Hegelian parentage, has never stood still. That makes it particularly difficult to do more than summarise its most essential principles in a book such as this.

5

MARXIST PHILOSOPHY

The revolutions of 1848 were a turning-point in European history. From Spain to Poland the Continent was torn by civil war as liberals and nationalists struggled for democracy and independence. The working-class, still a minority, played only a subordinate role, acting, as in England, as the radical wing of the liberal revolt. After 1848, as industry developed across the Continent, independent working-class organisations also spread, this time as the opponents instead of the allies of the middle-class of commerce and industry. The new master was the capitalist, and to many workers he seemed worse than those overthrown by the democratic insurrections. Eighteen-forty-eight, in fact, was the year in which the modern socialist movement, based on the class struggle against industrial capitalism, really begins. In Europe, at least, that development was given direction and coherence by Marxism.

Both Marx and Engels played a part in the revolution in Germany, but, when the movement failed, went into exile for the rest of their lives. German liberalism was too weak to succeed. Its leaders, moreover, were so fearful that their victory might open the way for the socialists that they preferred to make a compromise with the Junkers and bureaucrats rather than press their revolt too far. We have already seen how, in France, the Right had chosen to shoot down the Paris workers in thousands rather than share the fruits of the struggle with them. This action taught the moderate reformers in Germany a sharp lesson. Elsewhere in Europe the revolutionaries were too preoccupied with winning national freedom to bother much with social questions. Where they did, land reform seemed more important to them than the agitation of a handful of socialists in countries where the peasantry predominated, and there was no working-class in any real sense.

In none of the struggles of 1848 did the initiative lie with the working-class. Nevertheless, apart from the political experience gained by the workers, there was one development which completely transformed the character of socialism.

Marx and Engels, in emigration, had been brought into close contact with the secret societies and clubs formed by socialists and communists—many of them refugees from Germany—in Paris, Brussels, London and a few other towns. Among these groups was one called the League of the Just. During 1846 and 1847 Marx and Engels had won over the majority of the League to their way of thinking, and it was reorganised as the Communist League. At the end of 1847 they were instructed to draw up a programme for this body. In a few weeks the work was done, and the *Communist Manifesto* was published early in 1848.

It has been the most influential single document in the history of socialism, circulating up to our own time in millions of copies and translated into almost every language. For the first time it provided a basis upon which the socialist movement could be built as an organised and coherent party, as distinct from the sects and conspiracies into which it was divided up to and during 1848. It set the day-to-day experiences of the working-class against the background of history and gave them a meaning. It showed that proletarian misery was the result of a social system, not of the tyranny and evil of particular men; that this system could be changed only after a period of hard organisation and propaganda, culminating in the overthrow of capitalism by force; that reckless conspiracy was as futile as the utopian belief that capitalists could be persuaded to change their ways either by reason or example; and that the only hope of emancipating the workers from economic slavery was the activity of the workers themselves. Above all—and this is undoubtedly the secret of its influence—it was aimed less at providing an answer to immediate problems than at setting out a philosophy which would be a valid guide to the working-class up to and even after the day when it finally seized power. Marx and Engels certainly developed and revised some of the ideas which are put forward in the *Communist Manifesto*, especially on the side of analysis, but its scope is so wide and its picture of social development is so penetrating that it has been retained as a classic theoretical text for the socialist movement up to the present.

What did Marx and Engels say in the *Manifesto* and in their later writings which, for convenience, may be taken with it at this point?

History, they said, was not a succession of accidental events but a continuous process of social development according to a definite pattern. This conception they took from Hegel. With it they adopted Hegel's dialectical philosophy which stated that all change is the result of conflicts between diametrically opposed forces, which, in negating each other, produce a new and higher synthesis. For Hegel this took place primarily on the plane of ideas. Marx, on the other hand, applied this principle to human society. In a famous phrase of the *Manifesto* he declared that history consisted of class struggles. Every society is based upon a definite system of production. The character of that system, the way in which wealth is produced—by slaves, serfs, peasants or factory workers—determines the social and political pattern of that society. In every society, moreover, there is a ruling class which owns the means of production.

But new productive techniques develop, offering the prospect of increased wealth and command over nature. With them develop new classes which demand changes in social and economic organisation, at the expense of the old class of rulers. One mode of production becomes obsolete and a fetter upon the development of society. The class associated with the new methods endeavours to break down the restrictions upon their proper employment, and it is thus brought into direct and revolutionary conflict with the property relationships and with the State power of the old ruling class. This, for Marxism, is the law of social evolution.

In Western civilisation, Marx said, slavery had given place to feudalism, since the latter used the material and labour resources of society more efficiently. At the close of the Middle Ages feudalism itself had become a brake on economic progress. The merchant class, the bourgeoisie, fought the feudal aristocracy to break down the restrictions upon the use and expansion of wealth, to substitue wage-labour for serfdom, free enterprise for the stagnant medieval economy which was unable to take advantage of the opportunities offered by an expanding commerce, and by the discovery of the New World. Since it was based on a dynamic and developing system of production, the bourgeoisie was bound to triumph in the long revolutionary struggle—of which both the English Civil War and the French Revolution were a part—to clear away the remnants of feudal life from ground on which industrial capitalism was later built.

But as the economic foundations of society changed, so also did the property relationships, the political ideas and institutions, even the religion and the culture. Thus the whole range of man's social activities was raised to a higher and more complex level. This, however, did not mean that capitalist society was either stable or enduring, though Marx continually insisted that it was the most advanced form of social organisation that was possible for a long period in history. There would come a point, he argued, at which capitalism would, in its turn, be obsolete and bar the progress of humanity towards a richer and more prosperous society. Technical and economic development, Marx saw, would open new perspectives to man, would awaken hopes which capitalism would be unable to satisfy without destroying the very methods of production and exchange on which it rested. Unable to advance any further, having completed its mission, having knit the world into an interdependent economic system, capitalism would break up in a series of wars and revolutions. Once again a new class would rise to power, establishing a different system of production, novel forms of government, a fresh set of values and ethics. Just as the bourgeoisie developed the democratic ideology in its revolutionary youth, so this new class, the proletariat, would have its own philosophy, socialism. Marx believed, however, that the destiny of the working-class was to introduce a new kind of society in which, after some time, there would be neither opposing classes nor poverty.

Why did Marx state with such conviction that capitalism would disintegrate and that the proletariat would desire and be able to conquer power?

In the first place Marx realised that there was much more to the capitalist system than many of his contemporaries understood. For them it was certainly an immoral and inequitable method of controlling the productive resources of a country. But they would not grasp the significance of the changes that were taking place within the structure of capitalism as the nineteenth century wore on. The inherent tendency of capitalist industrial enterprise, said Marx, is towards monopolistic control, towards larger and more efficient plants, thus eliminating unnecessary competition between the producers. As capitalism extends its scope, this process is repeated on an international scale. Inside a country individual firms compete for a market, seeking the maximum profit for themselves and the bankruptcy of their rivals. In the same way, capitalist nations strive to gain control of as much of the world as they can, both as a source of raw material and as a market for their products. This imperialist drive leads inevitably to war, since each capitalist State must try to be more powerful than its competitors. Capital cannot lie idle: it must expand or perish.

Secondly, capitalism changes the character of labour. It is a condition of industrial production that it must draw together large numbers of workers under the same roof, in the same firm, in the same industry. The worker is no longer an individual: he is a unit in a process which is based upon collective effort. His personal fate is no longer dependent upon his ability to wrest a living from a plot of land or to turn out goods by hand in a small workshop. He is increasingly divorced from either ownership or direction of the means of production on which he relies to earn his keep; his condition of life is determined by events beyond his control; by, for instance, price fluctuations on some distant exchange or by the development of new techniques.

Yet the further this process goes, the more it unites the workers into a coherent and self-conscious class. In a particular factory they combine against a single employer; in an industry, against a group of them. From this it is but a logical step to unite against capitalists as a class and private enterprise as a system. Moreover, modern capitalism, at the same time as it increases the rivalry between nations, makes them more dependent upon each other. Since capitalism is an international system, it is natural and necessary that the workers, who have similar experiences and aspirations in all countries, should also organise internationally. Production, Marx understood, had changed from a handicraft to a social function. He saw that the more powerful private ownership became, the more it socialised the processes of production, drawing into an integrated whole ever-wider circles of the population. Therefore, he argued, a stage will be reached where the social character of industrial activity will conflict with its direction by one class of the community. Society is then ripe for radical change. Its social and political relationships must be reorganised to correspond with the socialisation of its economy. This is something that cannot be done until power has been wrested from the bourgeoisie and ownership of the land and factories transferred to the State. Marx, however, always insisted that the workers could not seize power until this point of crisis was reached. As long as capitalism was an expanding system, not having exhausted the possibilities of development within itself, it would survive. As soon as it began to contract it was a sign that its day was over and that it would have to make way for a new system.

The striking prophecy that capitalism would, indeed, enter a period of decline, made at a period when it seemed all-powerful, was the third reason that Marx advanced for his belief in the ultimate victory of the working-class, though he undoubtedly expected this victory at a comparatively early date, in his lifetime. It was based upon a lifetime's study of the inner structure of capitalist enterprise. The basis of Marxian economics was not new.

We have already seen how a group of early English socialists had taken Ricardo's argument a stage further and developed the theory that labour was the sole source of value. Marx placed this concept at the centre of his analysis. The worker, he said, by his labour, creates the value of a product. But he does not receive in wages the full equivalent. The difference between what he is paid and what the product may eventually fetch for his master, after other production costs have been met, is what Marx termed 'surplus-value', the source of the rents, interest and profits upon which the class of capitalists exists.

Since there is a gap between the total value of production and the purchasing power distributed in wages and salaries—and this gap is extended by the sharp gradations in the income-structure of capitalist society, and by the character of investment methods—capitalism, over a period, is unable to sell all the goods it produces. The more that the share of labour is reduced, or, at least, frozen in relation to the expansion of production, in the search for lower costs and higher profits, the greater the difficulty that capitalism encounters in finding markets. For a time this problem can be solved by selling manufactures to less-developed peoples. But, as capitalism brings more nations within its scope, industrialism appears in these countries and they become competitors. The capitalists of the more advanced States, by the export of capital, themselves promote this rivalry. The rate of profit all capitalists secure thus tends to fall on average. They are, therefore, driven, on the one hand, to reduce costs by improving technique or by lowering wages, or both, and on the other to try and exclude their rivals from definite markets, spheres of influence and colonial territories.

These processes lead to increasing inability to postpone a crisis within any capitalist system and, between competing systems, to imperialist struggles. By the time the world is divided between a few powerful imperialist States, the general crisis of capitalism will begin. Internally, it will be unable to overcome the gulf between production and purchasing power; abroad, the attempt to secure markets can only lead to world wars unequalled in their scope and cost. The epoch of the proletarian revolution has arrived.

Marx, however, was not a fatalist. He did not believe that the downfall of capitalism would lead inevitably to the victory of the working-class. Men, he insists continually, make their own history, and within certain limits set for them by the conditions of their time have a considerable amount of free choice. Therefore it is necessary to work actively for the socialist cause, not to wait until the millenium arrives of its own accord. Though the working-class may be brought into conflict with capitalism as a result of its social experience, the consequent protest must be organised into a coherent force. There can be a class-struggle which never results in the triumph of the pro-letariat because it has not been canalised into organisation by leaders who understand the laws of social change. It is this that is the task of revolutionary socialists. By relating day-to-day developments to the whole historical movement for working-class emancipation, they can make the working-class conscious of itself as a class and of its role as the one group in society capable of leading humanity forward.

Trade unions, Marx argued, are the primary organisations of the workers, and arise spontaneously. Their activities are largely confined to economic and industrial matters, such as the level of wages or the regulation of working conditions. But, Marx said, the capitalist class against which trade unions organise controls the State and dominates the intellectual and cultural life of society. Therefore the workers must form a political party to match the efforts of the trade unions. This party would carry the class-struggle into every sphere, municipal and national politics, philosophy, literature, the courts, the armed forces and even religion. It would not be sufficient for it to catch the votes of the workers year by year until it secured a parliamentary majority—though Marx conceded that this might be possible in some exceptional cases—since if the bourgeoisie faced a mounting political and economic crisis it would be quite capable of suppressing both the workers' party and its own democratic institutions. The working-class movement must be prepared to overthrow the bourgeoisie by force, for it would never voluntarily yield the State power it fought so hard to secure and maintain.

Once this has been done the workers must set up their own State —Marx uses the famous phrase here: a dictatorship of the proletariat which will effectively prevent a counter-revolution and pave the way for the classless society in which there will no longer be any need for the State as an instrument of class rule. Men, for the first time in history, will then be really free. Society can enjoy peace, since neither class antagonism nor war will disrupt it. There will be a rapid increase in social welfare because industry and agriculture will be operated for service and not for profit. The only limits on production will be the scarcity of the earth's resources and the degree to which man is able to harness them to his own ends. Both Marx and Engels were convinced that limitless opportunities of advance lay before mankind once its energy was no more squandered in social struggles and was devoted to the proper and extended use of its great technical discoveries. For them the victory of socialism marked the day on which the childhood of the human race would end and, conscious of the laws of science and society, men would begin to work together in a creative unity for their common prosperity and fulfilment.

This remarkable philosophy, of which only a bare outline has been given here, has been the most important single contribution to socialist theory. If much of it is accepted as commonplace today, that is a measure of the way Marxism has influenced the views we hold about the development and pattern of contemporary society, just as Darwinism revolutionised our concept of nature.

It is customary, today, to regard Marx primarily as the father of the modern communist movement—to accept the revision of his ideas by Lenin, Stalin and Mao Tse-tung as Marxist orthodoxy. But it is arguable whether Marx or Engels would have recognised totalitarian communism as the true heir to their philosophy. There are, indeed, many ways of interpreting Marx, and the Leninist reading is only one of them. Even in the nineteenth century, as we shall see, it was far from clear what 'orthodox' Marxism meant; today while we can note how much the socialist movement has owed to Marx, it would be sterile to insist that one reading is more 'correct' than any other.

6

THE YEARS OF FRUSTRATION

The years after 1848 were a difficult time for European socialism. The working-class groups had failed to take the initiative from the middle-class parties or to make any serious impression on the course of events during the revolutionary upheaval. Many of the leaders were driven into exile. Those who remained behind were either in prison or escaping the attentions of the police, and they had little opportunity to rally their disorganised and disillusioned supporters. In England, the Chartist demonstration of April 1848, which the Government had feared might be the signal for a revolt, ended in a fiasco which finished Chartism as a mass movement. The socialists in emigration spent their strength in hatching wild schemes for fresh insurrections, in recrimination about their failures, and in doctrinal controversy. It took the movement twenty years to recover from the setbacks of 1848. Throughout those years, it is true, there was an undercurrent of activity, but until the lessons of 1848 had been assimilated no headway could be made. The changed political and economic conditions in Europe required different methods from those which the old ideas and leaders could offer. Until they were pushed to one side, and until the further development of industry had produced another and more class-conscious generation of workers, the movement was doomed to be politically ineffective. Socialism, in fact, had to make a fresh start. It was only in the early 'sixties that this became possible.

Although the agitation of Ferdinand Lassalle in Germany after

1862, and the foundation of the International Workingmen's Association in 1864—the body now called the First International—were the first real signs of revival, some important work was done by the men who kept socialism alive in the years of stagnation. Most of them were in London, where political refugees from almost every European country had gathered. Together with a small group of Chartists who had belonged to the revolutionary wing of the movement, they tried to keep an organisational nucleus going against the day when mass activity would once more be practicable. Of course, this work was hindered and diverted by factional disputes.

But for all their weaknesses, the socialists in London did their best to carry on. For a while both Marx and Engels refused to play any part in *émigré* politics, for they were disgusted with its petty squabbles and futile intrigues. But, as the memory of 1848 faded and some of the more tiresome people dropped out or emigrated to America, they both worked actively with the revolutionaries in London, and gradually, as the influence of Marxism grew, became the two outstanding figures in international socialism. Their life in emigration was not easy. Engels, it is true, rose to be a most success-ful business man, but he had to support the Marx family most of the time. He did this willingly so that Marx would be free to devote his energies to study and political work. He modestly regarded this as one of the ways in which he could best contribute to the develop-ment of the philosophy and the movement to which they both gave their lives.

Engels, however, was not the passive colleague of Marx. He took a full share in the their joint theoretical work, and after Marx died he not only went on with his own writing, but he also edited two further volumes of *Capital* from the notes that Marx had left. The partnership of these two men, in thought and in action, was remark-able. There have been few friendships so intimate or fruitful.

Both Marx and Engels were organisers as well as thinkers. Their literary studies were pursued not as ends in themselves, but as practical assets for the political struggle. Early in his career Marx used a phrase that might have served as a motto for them both. 'The philosophers have only *interpreted* the world in different ways,' he wrote; 'the point, however, is to *change* it.' By 1848 Marx knew what his interpretation was. With some success he set about changing the world.

The work of the First International was the greatest practical achievement of Marx himself. But while he was the moving spirit behind it, he was not its founder. From some accounts, indeed, it would appear that it was created almost by accident. On the contrary, the International was preceded by a number of attempts to form an international working-class organisation, without which its own efforts could not have met with such success.

The English workers had shown sympathy towards revolutionary movements on the Continent as early as the agitation for the Reform Bill. Later, Chartist newspapers such as the *Northern Star* had encouraged the idea of international solidarity and had given a good deal of their space to reports of developments abroad, while foreign refugees took part in many Chartist demonstrations. In 1845 the Society of Fraternal Democrats was set up to act as a clearing-house for international information. It included representatives from almost all the countries in Europe. George Julian Harney was among its foremost members. It was not a separate party but a propagandist body, based on a communist platform which denounced national prejudices and declared that all men were brothers and equals.

By 1847 the Fraternal Democrats were well known outside England, and many of the foreign democratic papers reprinted their manifestos. In the last months of 1847 Marx arrived in London from Brussels to discuss with them the possibility of holding an international workers' congress. Harney had suggested this idea. It was frustrated, however, by the confusion of events in 1848. But, more than eighteen months before the slogan 'Workers of all lands, unite!' was given immortality in the *Communist Manifesto*, Harney was saying the same thing to the socialists in London. Harney and Ernest Jones, one of the younger Chartist leaders who also became a communist, were members of a delegation which visited Paris in March 1848 to greet the French revolutionaries.

After 1848 the Fraternal Democrats declined in strength and influence. With the collapse of the proletarian groups on the Continent and the drift of the English workers away from politics into co-operation and trade unionism, there was nothing to sustain such an international centre. Harney and his friends did their best to keep the Society alive by publishing numerous manifestos, by holding meetings on revolutionary anniversaries, and by collecting money for refugees in want, but by 1852 the Fraternal Democrats were forced finally to disband. Harney himself gradually dropped out of active politics.

This work was carried on, however, by Ernest Jones. After he had served a prison sentence for Chartist activity, Jones tried to rally some of the old revolutionary elements around him. Though he had little success in this, he became the chairman of a new body called the International Committee, on which sat representatives of the refugee groups in London. This organisation, like the Fraternal Democrats, issued a number of manifestos and called commemorative gatherings. But its outlook was much more confused. Deprived of the chance to do really effective political work, the exiles and their English associates fell back on empty rhetoric. Their public statements were full of revolutionary abstractions and vague but rolling phrases. The slogans of 1848 were repeated on every possible occasion without any apparent understanding that times had changed.

In April 1856 a delegation of Paris workers arrived in London to discuss the formation of a Universal League of Workmen which would unite the workers of all countries against international capital, and thereby secure their social emancipation. The Frenchmen, strongly influenced by the ideas of Louis Blanc and Proudhon, wished to impose a levy on twenty million workers throughout Europe, using the money to set up a network of producers' and consumers' co-operatives which, by their superior efficiency, would drive private capitalism out of business. Among those who took up this utopian project was the former Chartist leader Bronterre O'Brien.

Of course, the scheme was a failure, but it had a stimulating effect on the International Committee, which issued a manifesto stating that it proposed to expand into an international association open to members in all countries, with separate local committees in as many cities as possible. It would seek to recruit individual members who would be entitled to a vote at both national and international congresses of the organisation. This proposal, like that for the

Universal League, came to very little, though the International
Association apparently succeeded in making contact with supporters
in Europe and in America.

But it is worth noting that the form of the organisation was almost
an exact anticipation of the structure of the First International. In
fact, when another French delegation attended a meeting in London in
September 1864, from which the initiative came for the formation
of the First International, this was nothing particularly unusual. For,
all through the years in which socialism made little headway as a
mass movement, there had still been meetings called to affirm the
idea of international proletarian solidarity. Only two years elapsed
between the dissolution of the organisation led by Jones and the
establishment of the new and more successful International Working
Men's Association. To its founders, indeed, the latter probably
appeared as the direct continuation of the pioneering work of Harney
and Jones. But the First International was far more effective than
anything they ever did, though it owed much to their efforts.

The reason for this is not hard to find. By the 'sixties the recovery
of the movement on the Continent made it possible to set up an
international organisation which could secure genuine backing. The
predecessors of the International, struggling against the stream, were
primarily collections of sectarian refugees and old Chartist leaders
who increasingly lost touch with the workers they were trying to lead.
But the International did not depend very much upon these people.
It was able to tap the new forces that were emerging in Europe and,
for a time, to weld them together for common purposes. It therefore
became a body which was far more mature and influential than anything which had appeared up to that point.

Nothing better illustrates this change than the character of the
English trade union leaders, who played a large part in the formation
and work of the International. While they did not possess the fire of
the old stalwarts like Harney and Jones, they faithfully reflected the
new mood of the working-class. They had little use for inflammatory
speeches: they were more concerned with solving the immediate
problems created by the rapid and enormous expansion of British
industry. The hunger and unemployment of the Chartist days had
given way to a serious labour shortage. Apart from the demands of

the factories and the great construction enterprises like the development of the railways, millions had emigrated.

During this period trade unionism had taken a strong hold—
though it was now organised on a craft instead of an industrial basis
—and had thrown up leaders like Applegarth, Allan, Odger and
Cremer. These men were prepared to join in demonstrations in
favour of Polish independence or the abolition of slavery in the
United States, but one of the main reasons for their interest in international working-class action was their desire to exert some control
on the numbers of foreign workers who were arriving in England,
attracted by the industrial boom. The trade unions, which were
reaping the benefit of labour scarcity, were anxious to prevent cheap
foreign labour being used to drive down the rates they had so
laboriously managed to push up. Odger and the others had taken
steps to get in touch with French workers in 1863. In 1864 they
helped to found the International.

In France events were moving in much the same direction. Working-class discontent increased considerably after the economic crisis
of 1857 and the war against Austria in 1859, and socialist propaganda began to produce results. The most influential group was that
which supported Proudhon, at this time in exile in Belgium. Though
its programme included the usual demands for mutual credit
associations and denied the value of strikes and political activity, the
events of the early 'sixties gradually convinced the Proudhonists that
the workers should nominate their own candidates for the elections
to the legislative assembly, though, on the theoretical side, they still
kept to the original programme. Proudhon himself was won over to
this point of view just before his death. The Proudhonists, moreover,
were strongly represented in the delegation of French workers which,
under official auspices, visited London for the Exhibition of 1862
and made contact with English and German working-class leaders
there.

At this time two things were happening which drew the French
and English workers together. The first was the American Civil War,
which had a profound effect on the entire economic life of Europe.
Committees to help the workers who were unemployed as a result of
the dislocation of the textile trade were set up in both France and

England and communicated frequently with each other. The
working-class was also in enthusiastic support of the Union armies,
even when this support ran counter to their economic interests. The
second was the Polish insurrection. In the agitation to support the
insurgent Poles, the French and English workers took a large share.
Again there was contact between the two movements on a matter of
common interest.

All this preliminary work culminated in the meeting which was
held on September 28, 1864, to receive the reply of the French workers
to the fraternal message addressed to them almost a year before by
Odger and the other English leaders. Tolain, speaking for the
French delegation, successfully urged that an international organisation of workers should be immediately set up.

But the committee that was appointed to further this project had
no definite instructions. It consisted, moreover, of several national
sections which had no similarity in outlook. The English representatives included former Chartists and trade unionists; the Poles were
concerned with little but their own national problems; Mazzini, the
republican, led the Italians; Marx, like the other Germans with him,
was an old member of the Communist League. When efforts to
produce an agreed constitution failed, the task of making another
draft was given to Marx, who, by making a number of concessions
on points which he considered immaterial, managed to steer his
version through the committee. The First International was born.

The Inaugural Address of the International was a brilliant effort
to put the communist outlook in a form which would be acceptable
to a number of working-class organisations, each of which was in
an early and different stage of development. Marx, on the basis of
his exhaustive study of labour conditions and the structure oi
capitalist society, put forward a number of propositions on which he
believed that all these groups could unite. Reviewing the changes
that had taken place since 1848, Marx insisted that the gulf between
the workers and the bourgeoisie was widening in spite of the great
increase in wealth. He criticised the idea of superseding private enterprise by co-operative production on a national scale, pointing out
that the ruling class would use its political power to prevent such
usurpation of its economic privileges. The first duty of the workers,

therefore, was to form political labour parties all over the world, as a means to the conquest of power by and for themselves. Lacking a national and international organisation, the workers could achieve nothing; united they could overthrow the capitalists and transfer the control of production to society as a whole.

Though each section of the committee was inclined to take a different interpretation of these points, Marx was able to incorporate them into the Constitution of the International, as well as express them in the *Inaugural Address*. He did this so brilliantly that some of his phrases were literally transcribed into the programmes of many later working-class parties, particularly in Germany.

The technical preparations completed, the provisional leadership was anxious to hold the first congress and get on with the work of the International. But things were not quite so simple as that. Though the movement was reviving all over the Continent, there was still a great deal of political and organisational confusion. It was clear that before the International could begin to lead the workers of the world it was going to have some difficulty in persuading them to unite.

7

THE FIRST INTERNATIONAL

In the course of its comparatively short life the International became the terror of the ruling classes of Europe, though, in spite of its considerable achievements, it was never as powerful as they imagined. It was not a disciplined and unified body which unquestioningly accepted the revolutionary doctrines of Marx, but a federal organisation which only survived with difficulty a series of factional disputes on both theoretical and practical issues. All the same, Marx was the dominant influence in it, and most of the time he managed to carry a majority of delegates with him in the controversies provoked by the followers of Proudhon, and later by Bakunin and the anarchists. He succeeded in holding the International together because he understood how far and how fast he could move the limited forces at its disposal. He was not prepared to compromise on anything he believed to be a matter of principle, and he was a resolute opponent of the utopian and extremist schemes put forward by some groups in the International on the grounds that they would quickly lead to its complete disintegration.

While Marx was an expert tactician, however, he was able to do very little about the failure of the International to strike any strong roots in Germany. He was personally concerned with this problem, since it arose in part from the split between the group which looked to him for leadership and that which supported Ferdinand Lassalle, the founder of the German workers' movement.

Lassalle had worked with Marx and Engels in the Rhineland during the revolution of 1848, and was one of the first persons to study and adopt their philosophy of historical materialism. When his friends were forced into exile, Lassalle remained in Germany and spent most of the next ten years in prosecuting a sensational lawsuit. Though he kept in touch with the exiles, he did almost nothing in the way of politics. His relations with Marx cooled gradually, but there was an open breach between the two of them over Lassalle's attitude to the French war against Austria in 1859. He ardently desired the national unity of Germany—indeed his nationalism was as powerful a motive of his political actions as his socialism—and to secure it he was prepared to enlist the support of the Prussian ruling class. Austria, he believed, was the main obstacle, and therefore he hoped for a French victory.

Marx and Engels, however, insisted that the unification of Germany by Prussia would be worse than no unity at all. They saw a danger of Russian intervention on the side of France, and in that event hoped for a revolutionary war of the German peoples in which the progressive elements would come to the fore and both unify and democratise the loose confederation. Whatever the merits of the diplomatic argument, it revealed a difference in outlook that was to become increasingly important. If, in 1859, Lassalle thought that official Prussia was the one force which could effectively unify Germany, it was only logical that he should later be ready to believe that Bismarck could be persuaded to introduce the social changes which the middle-class seemed incapable of achieving. The degree to which the German workers' movement was influenced by nationalist sentiments is worth noting at this stage. For, in the next three generations, the readiness of large sections of the movement to subordinate their 'class', or socialist, aspirations to the interests of a united fatherland was frequently decisive. Lassalle's blend of chauvinism and social progress became an attractive though dangerous formula. It was borrowed by intelligent conservatives outside Germany: it was applied successfully inside Germany at every critical moment, from Bismarck's time until the rise of National Socialism.

From the beginning of his agitation in 1862 Lassalle bitterly opposed the liberal groups with which he had previously been associated. To a committee which had been set up in Leipzig to organise a congress of workers Lassalle addressed his famous *Open Letter*. In this he urged the formation of an independent working-class party. The workers, he said, could look for no improvement of their conditions under the existing system; for the 'iron law of wages' proved that if higher wages were secured by one group of workers the wages of other groups would inevitably fall. He argued that the solution of the social problem lay in the creation of co-operative associations by a State based on universal suffrage, in which all workmen would receive the full product of their labour. This programme won over the Leipzig committee completely and in May 1863 the Universal German Working Men's Association was founded, with the one immediate aim of universal suffrage. For the next two years Lassalle travelled through Germany, speaking to great audiences of workers and laying the basis of a national proletarian movement for the first time. In August 1864 he was killed in a duel.

Lassalle was as vain as he was able. Much has been written about this erratic and brilliant personality which emphasises his weakness, but none of it can obscure his achievement in reviving socialist agitation in Germany after years of apathy and inaction. Unfortunately, there was no general agreement that he had set the working-class movement going again in the right direction. Almost at once Marx and Engels joined issue with the Lassallians. While they agreed with the demand for universal suffrage, they refused to endorse Lassalle's naive suggestion that, independent of anything else, it could rapidly place all power in the hands of the workers. Lassalle, they said, overlooked the important part that trade unions played in the class-struggle. Though he claimed to be a follower of Marx, he urged the establishment of co-operative associations as competitors with private enterprise within the framework of the capitalist State, whereas Marx continually insisted that the conquest of power and the elimination of capitalist production was a prerequisite of successful co-operation on a national scale. But, above all, the quarrel was due to a dispute about the attitude that socialists should adopt towards the progressive middle-class parties. Marx had no illusions about the liberals, but he believed that the working-class should support them whenever they came into conflict with Bismarck and Prussian reaction. Lassalle, however, who bitterly denounced the liberal democrats, was unable to see that the ruling-class of Prussia, the Junkers who were represented by Bismarck, was the real and most dangerous opponent of the weak socialist movement.

While Marx was much criticised at the time for his refusal to have anything to do with Lassalle's political activity, he was quite justified by facts which came to light many years later when the secret correspondence between Lassalle and Bismarck was published. Lassalle hoped that Bismarck would make far-reaching concessions, would permit the workers to organise freely, would give them the vote and assist them to form co-operative associations. In return, he was prepared to support Bismarck's diplomatic adventures and his campaign against the liberals.

This policy would certainly have made the workers' movement a cat's-paw of the most reactionary force in German politics. It was the main reason for the breach between the Lassallians and the Marxists. The latter's suspicions were only increased when, in the war of 1866 against Austria, Bismarck introduced universal suffrage in order to secure the support of the workers. This war, if he had lived to see it, would have been greeted enthusiastically by Lassalle, for it was waged to exclude Austria from the German Confederation and to secure the hegemony of Prussia over all the other German States.

After the death of Lassalle a serious split developed between Schweitzer, the editor of the party organ *The Social-Democrat*, and Wilhelm Liebknecht, an old and close associate of Marx and Engels. Schweitzer wished to go on working along the same lines as Lassalle, since he believed that the independent workers' movement would be crushed if it tried to oppose the liberals and Bismarck simultaneously. When he printed a series of articles which could justifiably be interpreted as a eulogy of Bismarck's policy, Liebknecht resigned his position on the paper. After this split there was no question of the Lassallians affiliating to an International in which Marx played a leading part.

The Lassallians, all the same. did not have a monopoly of the German working-class organisations. There was a large number of groups which had been originally formed as off-shoots of the Liberal

Progressive Party. Most of these were formed from Saxon and South-German workers who disliked the growing ascendancy of Prussia. Under the leadership of Liebknecht and August Bebel, the two most prominent figures in the early days of the mass Social-Democratic Party, these workers were gradually won over to Marxist socialism. The union of these groups, at its congress in Nuremberg in 1868, decided to join the International. The next year, at the Eisenach Congress, the Social-Democratic Working Men's Party was founded. Thanks to Bismarck's introduction of universal suffrage, both the Lassallians and the Eisenachers were able to secure a few seats in the Diet of the North-German Confederation.

When the International at last held its inaugural congress at Geneva in 1866, however, the only Germans present were the representatives of the *émigré* circles in Switzerland and England. Marx himself, who was finishing the first volume of *Capital*, was too busy and sick to attend. Instead, he prepared an elaborate brief for the delegation which travelled out from London. It was soon needed. Supporters of Proudhon were in a majority among the French at the congress, and they made a determined effort to capture the International. They wanted it to declare its opposition to strikes and trade unions and its support of co-operative production based upon the free supply of credit. The English and Germans would have none of this mutualist programme. Basing themselves on the brief supplied by Marx, but making verbal concessions to the French, who controlled about a third of the congress, they succeeded in defeating most of the Proudhonist motions, including one that sought to confine membership of the International to manual workers—which would have excluded Marx, among others.

The final decisions of the Geneva Congress, reached after a series of chaotic debates, were a considerable victory for Marx and those who stood with him. While they did not commit the International to socialism, most of the tactical demands upon which Marx hoped to unite its various sections were at this point included in the official programme. In spite of the opposition of the powerful group of French delegates, the congress carried resolutions demanding protective labour legislation and a shorter working day, and insisted that trade unions were essential as the organisational centres for the workers, whose only strength lay in their numbers and their unity, against the powers of capitalist society.

During the next two years the influence of the International increased rapidly. The Lausanne Congress of 1867, and that held at Brussels in the following year, made it quite clear that the International was a socialist body. Though compromises with the French followers of Proudhon were still necessary, they were gradually won over to the socialist argument for collective ownership of the land, transport and communication facilities.

By the time of the Brussels Congress the International was sufficiently important to attract a good deal of attention from the European Press. *The Times*, which devoted four leading articles to the proceedings at Brussels, wrote: 'It is not a mere improvement that is contemplated, but nothing less than a regeneration, and that not of one nation only, but of mankind. This is certainly the most extensive aim ever contemplated by any institution, with the exception, perhaps, of the Christian Church.'

The International was not always discussed in such moderate terms. It was more usually denounced as the sinister force behind every workmen's agitation or revolutionary movement. But its prestige was based rather on the potentialities of the cause it championed than on a realistic assessment of its strength. While it gave support to strikes in Paris and assisted the English trade unions by preventing the importation of cheap labour, it exercised only a very loose control over its affiliated sections in every European country. At no time, moreover, did it possess anything but the most meagre financial resources for the enormous amount of work it tried to carry on.

The International was never free from serious internal dissensions. Up to the Basle Congress in 1869 the Proudhonists were the chief opponents of the line followed by the leadership. At that congress, however, Bakunin and the anarchists took their place, and the International became a forum for the bitter factional struggle between Bakunin and the Central Council, which supported Marx.

Michael Bakunin, who spent the great part of his life as an exile from his native Russia, was one of the most extraordinary figures in the nineteenth century. Like Marx and Engels, he was influenced by the Young Hegelian group in Germany during the 'forties. In 1848, after he had associated himself with the attempt of the exiles in Paris to form a revolutionary legion to invade Germany, he fought in the Bohemian and Saxon insurrections. Arrested at Dresden, he was handed over to the Russian police and imprisoned. A few years later he escaped from Siberia and returned to Europe by way of Japan and America. Though he met Marx in London during 1864 and promised his support for the International, he spent the next four years in Italy and Switzerland, organising his own revolutionary movement. In 1868 he founded the International Social-Democratic Alliance.

The Alliance was dominated by Bakunin, who believed that Marx overestimated the importance of the working-class. Still thinking in terms of the conditions of 1848, he insisted that the intelligentsia, especially the students, was a much more revolutionary element in society than the uneducated workers, whose energies were taken up with the struggle for their daily bread. The Alliance was a conspiratorial organisation, in the tradition of the old secret societies. It expected its members to be atheists who would wage war on religion and the State with equal resolution. But, in spite of its predilection for revolutionary phrases, it was not based on a consistent socialist programme. Bakunin, anxious not to frighten away potential supporters, at this time confined himself to vague demands for political and economic equality.

When the Alliance asked for affiliation to the International as a separate body, retaining its own constitution and programme, this request was refused by the General Council, which was already suspicious of Bakunin's intentions. Its members were admitted only after the Alliance was officially disbanded. All the same, their loyalty to the International was questionable. Marx had well-founded suspicions that Bakunin had entered the International only to capture it for his own ends. Both of them sought the destruction of bourgeois society by a social revolution.

But Bakunin, who had no faith at all in the political organisation of the working-class, regarded Marx as an obstacle to the insurrection which, he believed, could be carried out only by the alliance of the revolutionary intellectuals and the most wretched and depressed elements among the workers. (Bakunin's formula may have been more valid than Marx's. Industrial workers have not made the communist revolutions; but intellectuals and poor peasants have done so in non-industrial countries.) Within the International he accused Marx and the General Council of seeking to lead the movement towards the new tyranny of bureaucratic State socialism instead of struggling for a new society in which there would no longer be a division between the rulers and the ruled.

Though Bakunin secured considerable support at the Basle Congress, it was only later that his anarchist opposition became a serious challenge to the policy and position of the General Council. In the next year there were other things to occupy the attention of the International. It had already discussed the danger of a Franco-Prussian war at its Brussels Congress, and, denouncing all war as systematic murder, had urged that the workers should declare a general strike.

In July 1870, without much warning, war actually began between France and Germany, and the workers of each country were unable to do anything to prevent it. The International had to be content with issuing a proclamation written by Marx in which both Bismarck and Napoleon the Third were blamed for the disaster, and the collapse of the French régime was prophesied. In a few weeks France was, in fact, defeated and Napoleon himself captured. A republic was thereupon declared in Paris and a new government set up to continue the war as best it could. In a second manifesto, written on behalf of the International, Marx urged the German workers to demand an honourable peace and the recognition of the French Republic; the French proletariat was advised to keep a close watch on the vacillating and untrustworthy middle-class republicans. Above all, Marx declared that Bismarck's annexation of Alsace-Lorraine would only lead to another war in which France and Russia would be allied against Germany.

Paris capitulated late in January 1871. Though the armistice terms permitted the National Guard to retain its arms, the new government at Versailles, which was dominated by the reactionary parties, was far more concerned to deprive the radical population of Paris of its weapons than to protect the national interests of France against the excessive demands made by Bismarck. On March 18, when an unsuccessful attempt was made to seize the guns of the National Guard, Paris rose in revolt. On March 26 the Commune was elected. It survived until the end of May, when the defences of Paris were broken down and thousands of workers butchered in the streets by the Versailles army.

The Commune was a spontaneous rising by the Paris workers, who were disgusted with the treachery, corruption and exploitation that characterised their rulers. Though the International was universally charged with responsibility for the revolt, it was unable to give either effective guidance or practical assistance to besieged Paris. Even inside the city the members of its Paris section, who sat on the Council of the Commune, were outnumbered by the supporters of the veteran revolutionary Blanqui, who was still alive but who was prevented from entering Paris.

Nevertheless, the International willingly assumed the task of defending the motives and actions of the communards against an unprecedented campaign of abuse and misrepresentation. Marx was well aware that the leaders of the Commune were guilty of serious errors—some of which had accelerated its defeat—but he did not allow these to blind him to its real achievement. The Commune, he insisted in his brilliant commentary *The Civil War in France*, was the first occasion in history on which the working-class had seized power. It was the prototype of the proletarian dictatorship which would one day undertake the transition from capitalist to communist society. It had abolished both the standing army and the police, and given arms to the masses. It had begun to break the power of the clergy, the allies of the rulers of France, by expropriating their property. It had intended to provide free and universal education. And, finally, it had broken the old bureaucracy of State servants by making all public officials subject to election or deposition at any time, and by fixing their salary at a figure no higher than that of a skilled workman. The Commune lived for only six weeks, but, said Marx, it 'will be commemorated for ever as the glorious herald of a new society'. It had a lasting effect, not only upon the generation of workers which had witnessed it but also upon the whole development of European socialism.

After the defeat of the Commune, however, the International began to disintegrate. At the same time as it had to devote a good deal of energy to assist the numerous communard refugees, it was faced with a campaign of repression in a number of important countries. This would have been less serious if the various sections of the international had presented a united front against their persecutors, but, on the contrary, the internal feud between Marx and Bakunin had been intensified by the experiences of the Commune, the anarchists claiming that these justified their belief in a spontaneous revolt which could abolish the old State and establish universal freedom without any need for the intervening period of proletarian dictatorship on which the Marxists insisted. The French labour movement was paralysed for some years by the repression which followed the Commune. In Germany both Liebknecht and Bebel were imprisoned. They had refused to follow the Lassallians in voting for war credits in 1870, they had protested against the annexation of Alsace-Lorraine, and they had declared their solidarity with the Paris Commune.

Though the followers of Lassalle had their share of persecution, the militancy of the Eisenach party, which alone was affiliated to the International, involved it in serious trouble. In England, for reasons which are discussed below, the trade unions withdrew their support from the General Council. Thus in the three most advanced industrial countries, on whose workers the International had depended for its chief support, its influence dwindled rapidly.

A fair measure of the relative importance of the working-class movement in each country in the days when the International was at its zenith is provided by the number of representatives that each section had on the General Council—though many of these were exiles in London and were nominal rather than effective representatives. There were twenty from England, fifteen from France, seven from Germany, two from Switzerland and Hungary, and only one each from Poland, Belgium, Ireland, Denmark and Italy. The events of 1871 changed all that. At the private conference which met in London that year the International could not muster even as many delegates as there had once been members of the General Council.

But the International did not collapse at once. There was another congress at the Hague in 1872 at which the anarchists were formally expelled, and it was decided to remove the seat of the General Council to New York, where it remained until the International was finally liquidated in 1876. In its last years the anarchist organisations, which had been re-formed into the Alliance, became increasingly powerful and outrivalled the International.

As the possibilities of effective action on the part of the International diminished, so the personal and theoretical disputes between the two rival movements became more bitter. In Spain and Italy, both of them backward countries without a large proletariat, Bakunin's doctrines found support. In 1873 there were risings under anarchist leadership in Barcelona, Seville, Cadiz and Cartagena, which were suppressed only with difficulty. Everywhere Bakunin was gaining ground at the expense of Marx.

But the decline of the organisation was not primarily due to the disruptive intrigues of the anarchists, as Marx and Engels believed at the time. The truth was that conditions were no longer suitable for the kind of work that the International sought to do. The working-class movement was not developing at a steady rate or following the same course in each country. On the contrary, there were important and growing divergences. In places such as Spain and Itaily, where industry was in its infancy and the only possible form of political activity was conspiracy followed by insurrection, the Marxist insistence on the necessity of forming trade unions and an independent workers' party had little appeal.

The workers in such nations, moreover, still retained much of the individualism of the peasant and readily listened to the anarchist ideas of Proudhon and Bakunin. Marx, though he always understood that the working-class had to adapt its tactics to the different social and economic circumstances of each country, placed the greatest emphasis, during the formative period of the International, on the problems which were common to the workers of all capitalist societies—the demand for shorter hours or for freedom of organisation—and preferred to leave the more specific national problems open until the parties fostered by the International were more mature.

After 1871 the position of the working-class parties varied so much from one country to another that they could not afford to concentrate on general issues at the expense of the local and particular difficulties they had to face. At first Marx sought to check the decline of the International by strengthening the authority of the General Council, but the more he tried to control the constituent sections from a common centre, the more he hastened the process of disintegration. Gradually he came to realise that the International had outlived its usefulness and that the socialist movement had entered a new phase in its development.

The life of the International was short and, in spite of some limited practical successes, it was never much more than a propagandist body. Yet it laid the foundation of the modern socialist movement. It was the platform from which Marx was able to speak with such effect that Marxism became the gospel of millions of workers in the next fifty years. It finally destroyed the belief that the workers could contract out of the miseries they endured in capitalist society by setting up co-operative communities, without any need for a political or economic struggle against the employers of the State they dominated.

And, by continually insisting that the working-class must seek its own salvation by the seizure of political power and the liquidation of capitalist enterprise, it gave a tremendous stimulus to the formation of independent workers' parties. These parties, insofar as they were based upon Marxism, were also spurred on by the conviction that they were identifying themselves with the course of history and that they would ultimately triumph, whatever obstacles they temporarily encountered. Just as Marx transformed the theory of socialism, so the International was largely responsible for the conversion of the movement from a collection of disunited and virtually utopian sects into a number of realistic and well-established parties. After the defeat of the Paris Commune, as the prospect of revolution faded, each of these parties went its own way, adapting the basic principles of socialism to the political conditions of its own country.

8

THE REVIVAL IN BRITAIN

The character of the labour and socialist movements in Britain has always differed radically from that of their European counterparts. They have been, in their modern expression, empirical movements which acquired theories slowly and almost haphazardly, rather than movements which were created to advance a definite ideology. Their history, therefore, is as much a history of organisations as of theories. Long before socialism became an effective political force on the Continent the English workers were familiar with the socialist doctrines of Robert Owen and his contemporaries, and in the course of the Chartist agitation they had even created a mass revolutionary party of their own. But in the middle of the nineteenth century, just as socialism was beginning to make some headway in Europe, the English working-class abandoned it and turned instead to trade unionism, to consumers' co-operation and to the support of the middle-class reformers. The break with the past was complete.

For almost thirty years, from 1850 to 1880, socialism played no part of any consequence in the labour movement of this country. The experiences of the Chartist period were forgotten. Marxism, which secured an increasing influence among the workers of Europe, was either ignored or else dismissed, by the few who took the trouble to notice it at all, as an obsolete and untenable philosophy which had no relevance to the conditions in England. Although, at the turn of the century, there was a socialist revival, both the structure and outlook of the Labour Party that eventually emerged from it

were a reflection of the political tranquillity and prosperity of
Britain. The constitutional reform of society rather than the
revolutionary seizure of power became the objective of British
socialism.

It was not accidental that this period of comparatively peaceful
and non-political development coincided with the years of British
industrial supremacy. Though the improvement in the standard of
life of the working-class in this period has often been exaggerated,
there is no doubt that the workers, especially the skilled artisans, did
share in the wealth that was pouring into Britain, and that this was
a material factor in reconciling them to the capitalist system. They
were forced, it is true, into some bitter and protracted industrial
disputes. But, on these occasions, they were always at pains to point
out that their quarrel was not with the employers as a class but with
particular individuals or groups which refused to grant the unions
the recognition they regarded as their due or the limited and specific
demands they made for wage advances, shorter hours or better
working conditions. Until about 1880 there was no suggestion that
the system itself should be challenged. On the contrary, some of the
trade union leaders were as enthusiastic as the employers in their
eulogies of free enterprise.

The history of the British Labour movement after 1850, therefore,
is primarily the history of trade unionism. But these unions were
very different from their Owenite predecessors, the remnants of
which struggled without much success to keep going under the new
conditions. Even before 1850 there were signs that a fresh outlook
was developing among some of the trade unions, but the first real
change dates from the foundation of a number of smaller unions in
1851. This was the first of a whole series of unions which grew up in
the 'sixties and 'seventies, catering almost entirely for the skilled
workers, which sought to minimise rather than provoke conflict with
the employers, to negotiate rather than to strike, to regulate the
supply of labour to their trades, to centralise authority and control
of union finances, and to provide considerable sickness and unemployment benefits for their members.

This new outlook was not accepted at once or without some
opposition—even the ASE was forced to retain the old Owenite

demand for the foundation of co-operative colonies in its constitution—but, under the leadership of a small group known as the Junta,
the success of these 'new model' unions was such that they became
the most stable and powerful section of the movement. Some of their
leaders, men like Odger and Applegarth, for instance, were willing
to sit on the General Council of the International, which for a
short time was the effective centre of working-class organisation in
their country, but they took little interest in the theoretical polemics
of that body. For them it was an organisation which helped to
prevent the importation of cheap foreign labour into Britain and a
means through which they could express their sympathy with
oppressed democrats or national movements on the Continent.

It is doubtful if they understood at first exactly what the programme
of the International meant. In any case, they severed their connection
with it after Marx had openly championed the execrated Paris
Commune, when it was clear the International had no more practical
help to offer them. They had always refused to dissociate themselves
from the radical section of the middle-class and, in spite of the
efforts that Marx made to persuade them to put forward a distinctive
proletarian programme during the renewed campaign for an extension of the suffrage in the 'sixties, they took the trade unions into an
alliance with the Radical reform movement. They justified this
decision partly on the grounds that it was a waste of the workers'
money to conduct an independent agitation and partly by insisting
that there was only a difference of degree and not of principle
between their views and those of reformers like Cobden and John
Bright.

This partnership was only the beginning of a long period in which
the working-class played no separate role in British politics. It was
drawn into the struggle between the Liberals and the Conservatives,
and it was left to individual workers to choose which of the two
traditional parties they would support. Though the unions continually
declared that they had no interest in politics, this only meant that
they saw no need to organise their members as a class with aims
quite distinct from those of other sections of the community. Whenever legal judgments or new laws threatened to withhold the right
of free combination, there was an attempt to send working-class

representatives to Parliament, but it was never intended that these representatives should form the nucleus of a socialist party. On the contrary, they were put forward to ensure that the workers should have someone to speak for them in Parliament, just as the doctors, lawyers, landlords and other groups had spokesmen there who looked after their special interests. In fact, when the idea that the trade unions should sponsor their own party was raised, it found no more bitter antagonists than among the working-men who had been elected as Liberals.

The working-class leaders of this type—though there were important exceptions among the textile workers' and the miners' leaders—became increasingly identified with the outlook of the employers and of the Manchester school of economics, which taught that the less interference there was with the operations of free enterprise, the greater the prosperity of capitalist and worker alike. These men publicly rejoiced in the harmony they had created between master and labourer. They were respectable. On occasion they were willing to trade the interests of the men they led for the friendship of their Tory and Liberal friends. As early as 1871, when Applegarth stood as a candidate for the London School Board— this was only a few months after he had resinged from the Inter- national—his Conservative opponent withdrew and donated twenty pounds to his election fund.

This same man was the secretary of the London Master Builders' Association, the organisation which Applegarth and his union had spent years in fighting. It was not that these men, as a rule, were personally corrupt in the sense that they were bought by the offer of money or office. They were convinced of the values of Liberalism. Their actions reflected the attitude of the skilled workers, who believed that they had more to gain by peaceful collaboration than by conflict with an expanding economic system. This outlook was encouraged by a large number of organisations, which, agreeing that reforms were necessary, argued that they could be secured by persuasion. It was said the more the workmen displayed their thrift, their moderation and their self-discipline, the more likely it was that they would be considered worthy of the franchise, of higher wages and shorter hours. They were urged to devote the energies that might otherwise have been diverted into politics to religious duties, to the consumers' co-operatives which were developing rapidly throughout the country, and to the extension of the friendly society functions of their unions.

It is also necessary to take account of the difference between the English ruling-class and its European counterparts. It was more intelligent and flexible. It understood that much was to be gained if it sought to conciliate instead of to suppress the organisations of the working-class. It was able, when the demand for social change became too strong to ignore, to satisfy it by limited concessions at the critical moment. This was possible, of course, because the rulers of England seemed secure against any challenge and because they were sufficiently rich and successful to afford sections of the workers a share in their prosperity. Class differences were also less rigid in England, and the strong Noncomformist tradition cut across classes and thus prevented a sharp cleavage along either religious or social lines.

Too much stress, however, can be laid on the benefits which the working-class as a whole secured from the policy of conciliation pursued by its leaders and on the tolerance of the British employers towards trade unionism. In fact, the rise in living standards in the last twenty years of the nineteenth century was due as much to a steady decline in commodity prices as to wage increases, which in most trades were erratic and slow. The unions, moreover, had to fight hard for recognition in spite of their lack of militancy. The Liberals, by an Act of 1871, gave them legal protection for their funds. They managed, in return for supporting the Tories in the election of 1874, to obtain a further Act which recognised their right to strike. But their position was never too sure and, as we shall see, they were eventually driven into independent political action by a renewed threat to their legal standing.

In the period of prosperity that lasted to the end of the 'seventies, the unions—backed by the votes of the workers who had been enfranchised in 1867—secured a number of successes. The engineers won the nine-hour day, the miners the safety provisions of the Mines Act of 1872, and the factory workers an improvement in their working conditions by the Act of 1875. But the advances made by the unions themselves were almost wiped out by the disastrous economic crisis that started in 1879. The crisis, which was largely due to increasing foreign competition, hit both industry and agriculture severely. It produced a radical change in the nature of British capitalism, for from this crisis dates the appearance of two phenomena which were henceforth to be inseparable from it—imperialism and mass unemployment.

Until Disraeli, by a stroke of political genius, had identified the glory of empire with the fortunes of the Tory Party by making Queen Victoria the Empress of India, nobody in England had realised the value of the overseas possessions. But, by the economic slump of 1879, the challenge of foreign rivals to British industrial supremacy began, among other things, to take the form of an increasingly bitter struggle between the Powers for colonial territories. This imperialist scramble, moreover, was accompanied by a stimulated wave of jingoism which did something to offset social criticism provoked by successive revelations of the conditions of the poor and unemployed. During the 'seventies there was an upsurge of the Radical movement, led by Joseph Chamberlain and Charles Dilke—who at one time seemed likely to launch a full-blooded republican campaign—and there is no doubt that this Radical propaganda played a considerable part in preparing the way for the later development of a distinctively British form of socialism, which finally took form in the Labour Party.

After the crisis of 1879 there was a revival of socialist activity in Britain. Henry Hyndman, a wealthy Radical who had become disillusioned with Liberalism, founded the Democratic Federation in 1881, later reorganising it as the Social-Democratic Federation. Hyndman converted the SDF to a form of Marxist socialism and began agitating for the creation of a large working-class party. At first the SDF spent its efforts on the unemployed, believing they offered a good field for revolutionary activity, launching a campaign of socialist propaganda which lasted until 1914. It rivalled the achievements of Robert Blatchford, the author of *Merrie England*, which sold a million copies, and his supporters grouped round the paper, *Clarion*, as the source of pioneering socialist education for many thousands of workers. But the SDF, for all its efforts, was never able to rally a

significant body of working-class support behind it. Its work in the
depression years, however, was not entirely fruitless.

At the end of the 'eighties a small group of able young trade
unionists, who had been won over to socialism by the Federation,
set to work to organise the unskilled workers. Led by Tom Mann
and John Burns, this 'new unionism', as it was called, won some
striking victories, especially in the great dock strike in 1889 in London. It differed from the craft unionism of the skilled tradesmen in
its insistence on a militant industrial policy and in its endorsement
of a programme of moderate social reforms such as the right to
work, the eight-hour day and the municipal ownership of public
utilities, but it was equally unwilling to accept the revolutionary
Marxism preached by the Federation.

There are a number of reasons why the Federation remained a
small sectarian body. The most important was the reformist outlook
which dominated a majority of the workers. It was little use talking
revolution and class-war to a proletariat which was convinced that
its interests lay in peaceful acceptance of capitalism. The most
prosperous and best educated workers, as we have seen, were completely dominated by the ideas of class-harmony so assiduously
preached by their leaders, employers and a host of religious and
political reformers.

The Federation, moreover, had very little conception of the
importance of trade unionism, which it regarded as a reactionary
force diverting the workers from the political struggle for socialism.
Instead of participating in and guiding the day-to-day activities of
the working-class, as Marx had urged ever since the publication of
the *Communist Manifesto*, it put forward a peculiarly dogmatic and
inflexible version of Marxism. It was not surprising that the workers
failed to see what relation this involved philosophy had to their
everyday problems. The leaders of the Federation themselves had
only a very limited acquaintance with the work of Marx and Engels,
and as often as not they only partially understood the fragments
they did read. They had no sense of tactics. Though some of them
were able leaders of the unemployed, they failed to relate their
Marxist ideology effectively to the mass movements they were seeking
to create. The Federation was also weakened by internal disputes,

particularly in its early days, when it served as a political home for
anarchists, radical reformers, revolutionary Marxists and anti-
parliamentary socialists alike.

As early as 1884 part of the Federation split away to form the
Socialist League. This break had the approval of Engels—Marx had
died in the previous year—and Eleanor Aveling, one of the daughters
of Marx, was one of the leading figures in the League. But the
League was not even as homogeneous as the Federation, in which
many of the self-styled Marxists remained. Some of the League
members had broken away because they disliked and distrusted
Hyndman, some because they thought that there was no point in
such a weak organisation trying to act as a proper political party,
and others because they had no faith at all in the value of parliamentary institutions or of palliative reforms. For a short time in the
'eighties the League carried on an independent agitation, but it
passed more and more under the control of its anarchist wing and
eventually the Marxists and parliamentary socialists abandoned it
and rejoined the Federation.

Although the League was even less successful than the Federation,
it had in William Morris a leader who was one of the most remarkable figures in the history of socialism in Britain. Morris, who was
an artist and a poet of extraordinary ability, was led to socialism by
his hatred of the squalor and ugliness of industrial capitalist society.
He wanted to make life rich and beautiful for all men, and believed
that this would be possible only when all things were shared in
common and men worked for the joy of creative effort instead of
selling their bodies and their souls to a master bent on profit at any
price. He hated a social system which made art and culture inaccess-
ible to all save those with wealth, and at the same time put such a
premium on the pursuit of riches that all standards of taste and
value were corrupted. Until the victory of socialism enabled man to
realise his full spiritual and intellectual capacities, he was convinced,
life for the majority would be narrow, sordid and colourless. His
romantic vision of a socialist England, *News from Nowhere*, was one
of the finest of all utopias, written in an imaginative and glowing
style that has lost none of its appeal.

But Morris was neither a dreamer nor a dilettante. He passionately desired to make his utopia grow out of the poverty and the hideous industrialism he saw all around him. No task was too big or too petty for him to tackle. He was ready to sacrifice his energies and his money alike to the socialist cause. He wrote books, poems and articles for the movement; he lectured all over the country; he even sold socialist tracts and papers in the streets. Outside his own artistic field, however, Morris was not much of an original thinker and he drew heavily on Marx for his political inspiration, though he was never able to get very far with the economic analysis of his master.

His socialism was primarily a fierce emotional protest and an assertion that fraternity and beauty were as vital to life as bread. Though he had a pretty clear view of historical materialism, Morris was content to leave the study of the dialectic and the theory of value to other minds more capable of dealing with them. Socialism, for him, was both necessary and possible, and that was enough to justify all his efforts to achieve it. While Morris learnt the conception of the class-struggle from Marx, he interpreted it to mean that the revolutionary seizure of power was the sole aim of working-class organisation. This led him, for a considerable time, into an attitude of outright hostility towards parliamentary action, and towards any kind of reformism. Both, he was sure, served only to divert the proletariat from revolution and to keep the detested system tottering on for a little longer. He drifted towards anarchism in his hope that communism would be established on the morrow of a successful revolt, without any need for a transition period.

As the prospect of immediate revolution faded—and it had never been bright—Morris realised that the tide of events was running in the direction of State socialism, though to the end of his life he remained sceptical of electoral reform. He feared that the socialist movement might sink into the morass of cautious respectability, might become so absorbed in pettifogging details of administration that a system of State-regulated capitalism might be mistaken for the spirit and substance of real socialism, of a society of practical equality. To the last, Morris remained an uncompromising revolutionary, struggling, as he said of himself, 'to set the crooked straight'. In artistic taste, as in politics, he was one of the great formative influences on modern England. The direct successes of this generous and lovable man were few: his indirect achievements have been varied and immense.

While Morris and Hyndman appeared to be in the political wilderness, their work had repercussions in the very place where they expected least results—the trade unions. The 'new unionism' had not only begun to change the outlook of the whole movement on industrial matters; it had also produced a new attitude to political activity. During the slump of the early 'nineties the new unions did not disintegrate like their predecessors which had tried to organise the unskilled workers. Their politics held their members together in much the same way as the vested financial interests had been a source of strength for the craft unions in difficult times. At each annual Trades Union Congress there was a growing minority which demanded that the unions should sponsor their own candidates for Parliament, while local organisations were formed in different parts of the country to support the idea of an independent working-class party. In the middle of the 'eighties the unions had actually set up a Labour Electoral Association which boasted of eleven Members of Parliament, but this group broke up when the Liberal Party undertook to include a number of Labour candidates in its list. For some years there was continuous friction between the sections of the trade union movement which supported the Liberals in return for the nomination of a handful of trade unionists in working-class constituencies, and the socialist organisations which insisted on putting their own men up against the Liberals whenever they thought fit.

The alliance between the Labour representatives in Parliament and the Liberal Party which provided them with a refuge was a further stimulant to those who wanted a separate party which was committed neither to the Marxism of the Social-Democratic Federation nor to the Liberals. At the end of the 'eighties Keir Hardie, the leader of the Ayrshire miners, had started a socialist movement in Scotland which regarded itself as an opponent of the Marxists. By 1893 he was able to call a conference in Bradford to form the Independent Labour Party, which was attended by over a hundred delegates from a variety of bodies.

Though this new party was not all that Hardie desired, it was a step towards a mass working-class party which was neither committed to the revolutionary aims of the Marxists nor dependent upon the charity of the Liberals for its existence. The immediate aim of the ILP, which was based upon a vague and moderate socialist programme, was to contest local and national elections. In this it did not meet with much success, though its leaders were perfectly willing to trim their slogans to the electoral wind. It was soon clear that the ILP, although it stood much closer to the position of compromise adopted by a majority of the workers than the Marxists, could not get sufficient trade union backing to become the kind of party Hardie wanted to build. He was seeking to form an alliance between the unions, which had the money and the membership to sponsor a large number of Labour candidates, and the socialists, who would provide a virile leadership. In 1899 a motion was passed at the Trades Union Congress instructing its Parliamentary Committee to call a special conference 'to devise ways and means for the securing of an increased number of Labour Members in the next Parliament'.

This conference met in February 1900 and there was an immediate clash between the representatives of the ILP and those of the Social-Democratic Federation, which had been invited to take part in the discussions. The ILP was more concerned with the formation of a Labour group in Parliament which would be distinct from the Liberals than with the programme of this group, believing that any attempt to foist a socialist policy upon Labour men who were reluctant to make any break at all with the Liberals would wreck the negotiations from the start.

The Marxists, however, asked what point there was in forming a new group if it was not given any definite political instructions. It was obvious, they said, that the group, though nominally independent, would continue to function as little more than an appendage of the Liberals. But the ILP proposal, which was put up as a compromise to offset the challenge of a far less socialist resolution, was carried, and the Labour Representation Committee was set up. In the elections of 1900 the candidates sponsored by the LRC, apart from Hardie and Bell, were defeated, though ten 'Labour' candidates were elected on the Liberal list. All of them refused to have anything to do with the LRC.

When, in the following year, a second conference was held, it was reported that the affiliated union membership of the LRC had increased only from 375,000 to 469,000, and that of a total of one thousand unions a mere handful had applied for affiliation to the LRC. At this conference another attempt by the Marxists in the SDF to tie the new movement down to a definite statement of principle was defeated. It looked as though the Labour Representation Committee was doomed to the same failure as its predecessors, and the delegates from the Social-Democratic Federation, disillusioned and suspicious, withdrew from it.

This defeatism was premature, for the whole position was changed by a new threat to the legal standing of the trade unions. Under the Acts passed in the 'seventies the union officials had been secured against criminal prosecutions, and it was assumed that, as corporate bodies, they also enjoyed immunity from civil proceedings to recover losses caused to the employers by strikes. In 1901, following a strike in South Wales, the Taff Vale Railway Company took the Amalgamated Society of Railway Servants to the House of Lords and was awarded twenty-three thousand pounds damages. This decision was a major disaster to the trade union movement. As long as it was allowed to stand it was almost impossible for a union to allow its members to strike for fear of being involved in ruinous legal actions. In self-defence the unions had to throw themselves into the struggle to reverse this judgment by legislation.

This crisis saved the Labour Representation Committee. In less than two years its affiliated unions numbered nearly two hundred, with a total membership of one million. These unions introduced a political levy on their members and devoted the greater part of the funds thus raised to the LRC. At the elections of 1906 the LRC put up fifty candidates, twenty-nine of whom were returned. For the first time the Liberal-Labour men were in a minority, only fourteen of them being elected. In the same year the LRC was reconstituted as the Labour Party, retaining its form as a federation of trade unions and socialist organisations, with its own party and not a mere group in Parliament. Among the latter was the Fabian Society, which had joined the LRC in 1900, and which was to become the dominant theoretical influence in the new party.

9

THE FABIANS AND THE LABOUR PARTY

The Taff Vale judgment forced the trade unions to affiliate to their own distinct Labour Party, but it did not suddenly convert them to socialism. Yet the new party required some sort of distinctive philosophy. It was obviously illogical for it to oppose Liberal candidates at the polls and still accept the traditional doctrines of Liberalism. It was even more illogical to expect that trade union leaders, fresh from the Liberal fold and devoted to constitutional reform, would pay any attention to the handful of Marxists in the Social-Democratic Federation. In the reformist socialism of the Fabian Society the young party found what it needed. The Fabian outlook has ever since dominated the socialist movement in Britain.

Unlike most other socialist organisations, the Fabian Society was never meant to do the work of a political party. From its foundation in 1884 it was intended to be a small propagandist body of intellectuals who, sharing a common desire for social reform, would try to secure the changes they sought through the agency of whatever individuals or organisations they could win, by persuasion or permeation, to their side. It was led from the beginning by some of the most brilliant minds of the time, notably George Bernard Shaw, Beatrice and Sidney Webb.

The tactics adopted by the Fabians were a direct reflection of their attitude to society. Although, until the local Fabian Societies merged themselves with the ILP, they did have fairly close contacts with some parts of the working-class movement, they were equally, if not more, ready to concentrate on permeation of the Liberal Party, which seemed the most likely sponsor for their detailed schemes of reorganisation for everything from slaughter-houses to railways.

Believing that society developed by a steady progression of small functional and structural changes, rather than by revolutionary leaps, especially where it is ruled by democratic methods, the Fabians naturally regarded every form that extended the scope of public ownership or control as an instalment of socialism, the socialist commonwealth thus being reached gradually and almost impercept-ibly. They rejected, in a somewhat summary fashion, the Marxist analysis of capitalism. Indeed, Edward Pease, the official historian of the Fabian Society, claimed that 'its first achievement . . . was to break the spell of Marxism in England'. In place of the labour theory of value, which had been the main analytical conception of socialist economics up to that point, the Fabians formulated a different approach to capitalism, based on 'economic science as taught by the accredited British professors'. According to the theories of John Stuart Mill, who may be regarded as the real parent of the 'British' theory of socialism, and of Jevons, on whom the Fabians drew heavily, there were natural laws of supply and demand which automatically ensured that the worker received the wage that was his due, that the capitalist had a reward for the use of his money, and that the community was provided with the goods and services it most required.

This doctrine of marginal utility, as it is known, was an extremely sophisticated justification of private enterprise. Though the Fabians did not accept the conclusions which the defenders of capitalism drew from this analysis, for they advocated the abolition of the capitalist system whose workings it attempted to explain, their own doctrine shows considerable evidence of its influence upon them. They sug-gested, however, that the origin of the unearned incomes of landlord and employers alike was the rent that they received from their owner-ship of the means of production and not, as Marx insisted, the sur-plus-value created by the workers.

It followed from this that private ownership was undesirable and ought slowly to be reformed out of existence. The Fabians did not believe, however, that there was any urgent reason why socialism should replace capitalism. Certainly, on moral and political grounds, they hoped it would. But, basing their analysis on the theories of the foremost capitalist economists, they assumed that society would not necessarily run into disaster even if the arrival of socialism were to be postponed indefinitely.

The attitude of the Fabian Society towards the working-class movement was a logical result of this economic outlook. It presumed that there was a growing indentity of interest between the employers and their workers; that living standards would continue to rise and unemployment diminish; and that socialism was the most rational form of social organisation which all reasonable men in the community could be persuaded to accept. In view of its failure to capture the Liberal Party by permeation and the evident reluctance of a majority of the employers to assist in their own painless liquidation, the Fabian Society associated itself with the demand for a separate Labour Party and then, having helped in the formation of that party, began to use it as the instrument for achieving the desired reforms.

But this did not mean that the Fabians had been convinced that their effort to secure social change by general consent could be established only by a working-class that spurned all collaboration with its exploiters and set out to dispossess them by the seizure of political power in the State that they controlled. On the contrary, the Fabians shared the prevailing view of radical reformers and of the dominant section of the men who formed the Labour Party that there was no clear division between capitalist and socialist society, that the one would step by step be transformed into the other by the process of legislative action. It was the duty of the workers to elect as many representatives as possible to Parliament, and to the municipalities, to assist that process.

By the constitutional methods of democracy the Fabians believed the land and the factories, the gasworks and the railways could be transferred from private ownership to the State. But their view of the State was very different from that of the Marxists. It seemed to them a completely neutral force in society. Its powers and functions, they thought, were at the disposal of any group that commanded a majority in the House of Commons.

It was, in a sense, an enormous version of a Government Department, impersonal and efficient. To ask, as the Marxists asked, what social class controlled the State and shaped its policy, was a meaningless question to the Fabians, who refused to accept the idea that society was divided into opposing classes. They saw the State as the centre of the administrative machine and denied, as far as they considered the matter, that it was also an instrument of class rule and coercion.

They did not, therefore, anticipate any difficulty in using the existing State to accomplish the transition to socialism; it appeared to be a neutral agency which could be used as easily for this as for any other purpose. There was no need to reconstruct it, as the Marxists asserted, to ensure that its structure reflected the new social conditions. Such alterations as were required could be made piecemeal as its powers were gradually extended. After a good many years had passed, it is true, the Fabians began to reconsider their judgment about the nature of the State. But they never discarded their conviction that in a democracy based upon universal suffrage the State was always at the disposal of the majority, or that the machinery of parliamentary democracy was eminently suitable for the establishment of socialism by consent.

The Fabians were primarily concerned with domestic and particular reforms, and in this they were responsible for some considerable achievements. They understood that they were more likely to get the things they wanted done if they concentrated their efforts upon definite and detailed proposals for handing water supplies over to local authorities, or eliminating anomalies from the system of poor relief, than if they dissipated their strength in trying to cover the whole field of international politics.

They consequently took very little notice of foreign affairs. When the Boer War broke out a Fabian manifesto declared that this was an issue 'which Socialism cannot solve and does not touch', though Bernard Shaw later published a pamphlet called *Fabianism and the Empire*, in which he justified imperialism on the grounds that an advanced nation had the right to conquer a backward people in the name of efficiency and progress. The Fabian Society reacted similarly to the outbreak of war in 1914, declining to make any statement of policy.

Socialism, in the Fabian sense, thus became a technique of legislative reform within the framework of a capitalist society. The task of the Fabians, as they conceived it, was not to overturn that society but to hasten, by piecemeal modification, its already evident drift towards collectivism. They were not particularly impressed by the Marxist analysis of the tendencies in capitalist development. They thought that Marx had been wrong in almost every prediction he made, and they summarily rejected his argument that capitalism would inevitably run into a series of catastrophic wars and economic crises.

Although the Fabian Society was never a large body—in 1906 it defeated a proposal made by H. G. Wells that it should turn itself into a national organisation with a big membership—it succeeded in imposing its views upon an increasingly important section of the Labour Party, and in 1918 its efforts were crowned with success and the party adopted a nominally socialist programme. As early as 1906, however, the secretary of the Labour Party, Ramsay MacDonald, had stated the principles upon which the new party was based in terms which reflected the influence of the Fabians. It must resist any attempt to present it purely as a movement of the workers, Mac-Donald said, for these principles were not reached 'by a process of economic reasoning or of working-class experience'. On the contrary, they rested 'upon conceptions of right and wrong common to all classes'.

This attitude was typical of the Parliamentary Labour Party in the years up to 1914. Its independent political activity was confined to issues about which the trade unions felt strongly and about which the Liberals were reluctant to do anything unless they were pushed; its socialism never went as far as the limits set by the Fabians, the only theorists it possessed. After the Liberal victory in 1906 a new Trades Disputes Act was passed to reverse the Taff Vale judgment; the eight-hour day introduced into the coal mines; old-age pensions, and free meals for school-children provided; and the system of workmen's compensation extended.

But the trade unions began to feel that all these things might have been done, anyway, by the Liberals, without any need for the expense and trouble of maintaining a Labour group in Parliament.

Their interest in the latter was obviously waning when yet another attack was made upon their legal rights. In 1909 the House of Lords decided in the Osborne case that it was illegal for trade unions to devote any of their funds to political purposes. Indeed, this judgment raised doubts about the legality of other activities of the trade unions, about their association in trades councils, and even in the Trades Union Congress. The unions once more rallied behind their own party to work for legislation which would remove the serious restrictions placed upon their activity by the Osborne judgment.

There was, however, a growing section of the trade union movement which wanted nothing to do with politics as practised by the Labour representatives in Parliament. Ten years before it had been the most radical workers who had demanded the formation of their own party and the moderate union leaders who had insisted that the movement should confine itself to industrial matters. These positions were now reversed. While their leaders were praising the virtues of legislative reform, the militant workers were preparing for direct industrial action on a large scale. It was by no means the unskilled workers only who were ready for a head-on conflict with the employers. In fact, the very unions who had previously preferred arbitration and the automatic adjustment of wages by a system of sliding scales, especially the miners, were willing to fight both their employers and their union leaders, taking the lead in the series of stikes that started about 1908. One of the main reasons for this change of front was the tendency of real wages to fall.

Up to the end of the nineteenth century, however money wages had fluctuated, there was a general and fairly steady rise in real wages due to the decline of commodity prices. In the first decade of the present century real wages were dropping again, and the workers realised that they could maintain their position only by considerable increases in money wages. They wanted these advances quickly, and were not prepared to wait for the lengthy processes of arbitration or accept the operation of old agreements which often provided for a reduction of wages at the very moment the workers concerned desired them to go up.

This new temper was responsible for many great strikes, dislocating the transport of a number of cities, the railways all over the country and coal production, to say nothing of scores of less spectacular disputes that accompanied them. In 1904 less than two milllon working days were lost in strikes; in 1912 the total was over forty million. A 'Triple Alliance' was formed by the transport workers, the railwaymen and the miners with the object of organising a general strike for their demands. Yet the rising curve of industrial unrest was almost entirely dissociated from the Parliamentary Labour Party, in which many of the strike leaders had little faith or interest, since they regarded all parliamentary politics as a diversion from the real struggle of the working-class.

In this struggle they believed the picket-lines rather than the polling-booths to be the scene of the fight against capitalism and the employers. Under the influence of French syndicalism (which is discussed below), and the industrial unionism in the United States, the extreme Left had abandoned all hope of salvation through constitutional reform and had turned to direct industrial action as the one effective means by which the workers could win control of industry. They despised the State socialism of the Fabians; they did not want mere nationalisation, as the famous pamphlet *The Miners' Next Step* explained. Strike action alone would push wages so high that it would be unprofitable for the employers to carry on. The workers themselves would then take over and operate the mines and the factories.

Accompanying this syndicalist agitation, though on a more sophisticated plane, was the propaganda of the Guild socialists. Their policy was as much a reaction from Fabianism on the intellectual level as syndicalism was from the role played by the Labour representatives in Parliament and the ideas of industrial harmony still supported by a part of the trade union leadership.

Some of the Guild socialists, such as G. D. H. Cole, for instance, had actually broken away from the Fabian Society. They did not believe, as the syndicalists believed, that the State and political action could be disregarded completely, at least for some time. Neither did they share the Fabians' conviction that the State was a neutral machine of administration and not the instrument through which a particular social class dominated the rest of society in its own interests. They disliked the State precisely as a machine of administration and desired to limit rather than increase its powers to direct production, distribution and people. The transformation of England into a socialist commonwealth, they thought, was a matter of changing its economic structure, without any need for the workers first to seize power.

Consequently, like the followers of Owen and Proudhon, who had been equally sceptical of the value of political methods, they sought to begin the transition to socialism by creating, within society as they found it, the kind of economic organisation they desired. Similarly, they concentrated upon drafting elaborate projects for the actual operation of the industries they proposed to socialise.

The Guild socialist movement sprang from a number of sources. Its leaders were greatly influenced by the views of William Morris and John Ruskin, both of whom had bitterly attacked the way in which capitalism had produced a cult of the machine at the expense of the individual's sense of craftsmanship and beauty. Seeking, as Morris had sought, to restore the dignity of labour, they turned for inspiration to the medieval self-governing guilds, in which they believed that men had been offered an outlet for their creative instincts. They wished to reverse the whole scale of moral and aesthetic standards which capitalism had imposed. The wage system, for the Guild socialists, was spiritually and economically intolerable for it both corrupted the personality of the worker and exploited him. Service to the community, they said, should be the only criterion of production; the idea of profit should be eliminated.

This was to be accomplished by setting up a number of National Guilds, each of which would be responsible for the operation of a particular industry. These Guilds would be organised nationally in a Guilds Congress which would have the same sort of control over the economic activity of the country as Parliament had over its political and foreign affairs. The Guilds would be self-governing, thus giving the worker an adequate chance to participate in the control of the industry in which he worked, and as a result an opportunity for the proper expression of his personality. Industries socialised in this fashion would be able to offer far better standards of payment—apart from the more intangible rewards—since the only interests that had to be considered would be those of the

D

producers and consumers who formed the community. There would be no idle rich or unearned incomes under Guild socialism.

In all this the trade unions were cast in a leading role. Since the processes of social change were economic rather than political, the Guild socialists considered, the unions—and these were to be industrial unions—were the most suitable instruments for creating the desired National Guilds. They could not do this, however, unless they realised that their functions could not be confined to securing mere improvements in wages and working conditions; they had to aim higher than that, endeavouring to abolish the system of wage labour entirely, and to take an increasing share in controlling the supply of labour, its reward and its part in the management of industry.

In general, the philosophy of the Guild socialists was far more radical and coherent than that of the Fabians. They were not content merely to wait until the slow accumulation of reforms carried England into a bureaucratic State socialism; they wished to undertake the transition as quickly as possible, even if it involved an extensive recasting of existing institutions.

In the new society there would be no single centre of authority able to direct every social activity without challenge. The Guild socialists wanted as much decentralisation of administration as of industrial management and control. Since they saw the State as but the largest of a whole series of bodies in which men came together for a common purpose—such as the churches, trade unions, political parties, and even recreational organisations, each of which contributed an indispensable element to the life of its members—they sought to give each of these bodies the fullest freedom to control its own specific activities as was compatible with any kind of order and unity within society.

Naturally, in their plan of things, they allowed the State to retain some of its powers, provided that these did not restrict unnecessarily the liberty of all the other associations, but they never accepted the view that the State, as such, had an overriding claim upon the services of its subjects, irrespective of their own feelings.

Guild socialism, however, did not become a mass movement, and though it survived throughout the war of 1914–18—the National

Guilds League was actually formed in 1915 after nearly ten years of propaganda by Orage, Penty and S. G. Hobson, who, with Cole, were the most prominent Guild socialists—it dwindled rapidly in the post-war years as the growing strength of the Parliamentary Labour Party enhanced the prospect of a Labour Government along the lines desired by the Fabians, and as the Left wing of the Guild socialists joined the communists.

Nevertheless, it did a good deal to revive controversy and to stimulate theoretical discussion about the *kind* of socialism which was practicable and desirable in England. Its appearance was, above all, a sign that the working-class movement in England was unable to get much further by repeating the old slogans and muddling on from one crisis to the next without any clear idea of where it eventually wanted to go. So far, it has not gone in the direction suggested by the Guild socialists, but their work did at least draw attention to the danger of regarding the transition to socialism as merely a matter of administrative reorganisation in the interests of efficiency. Like Morris, the Guild Socialists wanted a social regeneration.

10

GERMAN SOCIAL-DEMOCRACY

In the thirty years after 1870 the German socialist movement became the most powerful in Europe. Until the 'seventies, as we have already seen, it was split into rival sections, one under the leadership of Schweitzer, who had succeeded Lassalle, and the other led by Wilhelm Liebknecht and August Bebel, who were supporters of Marx and of the First International. In the elections of 1871 the two groups polled over a hundred thousand votes between them. This aggregate vote rose to 340,000 in January 1874, the Lassallians securing three seats in the Reichstag and the Eisenach faction winning six.

These electoral successes soon attracted the attention of the Reich Government, and both parties were faced with a campaign of persecution. In this difficult period they began to discover how much they had in common. Their representatives in the Reichstag had fought the elections on similar programmes and worked together for the same demands and against the same enemies. The legal existence of both parties was threatened by judgments secured by Tessendorff, the public prosecutor. The main obstacles to unity, in fact, were the memory of old quarrels and some theoretical differences whose importance did not seem to be very great compared with the practical difficulties confronting the two sections. In October 1874 negotiations for their fusion began.

For a time Liebknecht kept these negotiations secret from Marx and Engels in London. He did not attach so much weight as they did to theoretical matters, and he was perfectly willing to make very considerable concessions to the Lassallians in order to get them into the united party as quickly as possible. He knew that Marx was opposed to fusion for fear that the new party might fall into the hands of the numerically stronger Lassallians. Thus when Marx and Engels finally saw the draft programme upon which the two parties had agreed, it was too late for them to do anything. Though they protested in the strongest terms to both Liebknecht and Bebel, they secured nothing more than a few trifling alterations in the text. The programme was adopted by the unity congress that met at Gotha in 1875.

Marx and Engels denounced the programme as an intolerable compromise, but their criticisms were ignored in Germany. None of their supporters realised that the two exiles in London were not simply splitting hairs but raising extremely serious theoretical issues. To the men on the spot, who were chiefly interested in the practical benefits that would result from unity, it did not seem to matter much if the paper programme had to be watered down to meet the demands of the Lassallians. They did not understand that there was a major difference of principle between the views of Marx and those to which the programme committed the movement. The *Gotha Programme* paid no attention to trade unions; it denied the possibility of effective international working-class activity; and it took over the Lassallian conception of the State as a neutral instrument of government which could be directed, once the workers had an electoral majority, to socialist purposes. Marx, on the contrary, believed that if the movement accepted this reformist outlook uncritically, the workers would be diverted from their real task, which was to overthrow capitalism and the State associated with it.

But his critique made no impression on the leaders of the new party. It was clear that those who professed to be Marxists shared in the prevailing theoretical confusion. In spite of their respect for Marx and Engels, few of them had any idea of Marxism as a coherent and comprehensive philosophy. When, however, numbers of them began to turn to the wordy and pretentious arguments of a Berlin professor called Dühring, Engels decided that it was time he set down a clear statement of the principles of socialism for which he and Marx stood. He did not know that his polemical book *Anti-Dühring* was, in the long run, to play a decisive part in winning the socialist movement in Europe for Marxism. Yet this book stated in a lucid fashion just how Marx and Engels interpreted both the course of history and the events of their own day. It not only won over the most brilliant young socialists to Marxism, but the reprint of the political chapters, *Socialism, Utopian and Scientific*, was circulated almost as widely as the *Communist Manifesto*, with which it must rank in influence. It took some years for this work to accomplish the conversion of the German and other socialist movements, but there is little doubt that its publication marks the point at which Marxism began to establish its supremacy over other socialist doctrines.

Despite the theoretical dissensions inside the party, it made rapid headway. In the elections of 1877 it polled more than 500,000 votes and sent twelve representatives to the Reichstag. But its increasing strength brought it in conflict with the authorities, who determined to check its progress before the party was properly consolidated. Two unsuccessful attempts on the life of the Emperor in 1878 provided a suitable excuse for repressive legislation, although the party was free from all responsibility in both cases.

The Anti-Socialist Laws, which were passed at the instigation of Bismarck, almost broke up the party. Some of its leaders were exiled; it could neither hold public meetings nor publish newspapers. The only socialists who could speak with any freedom were the dozen members in the Reichstag. But a majority of these held that the only way to hold the movement together was to abandon the radical principles on which it was based and to co-operate with the progressive bourgeois parties. The minority, which included Bebel and Liebknecht, struggled hard to act as the spokesman of the persecuted revolutionary workers, who had no other legal means of expression.

In this period of illegality it was obviously necessary for the party machinery to be held together from abroad. It therefore fell to the exiles to organise the congresses of the party and to publish its paper, the *Social-Democrat*, thousands of copies of which were smuggled into Germany, first from Zürich and later from London. For most of this time the editor of the paper was Eduard Bernstein, who afterwards became the leading critic of Marxism inside the party.

While Bismarck had no hesitation about repressing the socialists, he was intelligent enough to realize that he could not destroy their influence unless the workers were compensated for the loss of liberty by social reforms. In 1882 he put forward legislation providing accident and sickness insurance. Old-age pensions followed. Bismarck was ready, as he had admitted in introducing the Anti-Socialist Laws, to accept a good deal of what had once been demanded by Lassalle, such as the nationalisation of transport, the equalisation of wealth through taxation, and the stabilisation of employment through State action.

Nevertheless, for all Bismarck could do, the socialists gained ground. In 1884 they polled 549,000; in 1887, 763,000. By 1890, in spite of the laws restricting their activity, they had become the largest single party in the Reich, securing 1,427,000 votes. It was clearly impossible to hold them in check by persecution, and the Anti-Socialist Laws were abandoned. The party then had to take stock of its position, after more than ten years, in which it had been unable to meet openly or provide for free consultation between the leaders and the rank-and-file. It was soon clear that the Marxists now dominated the party; at Erfurt in 1891 the party congress accepted their draft of a new programme to replace the old one which had been adopted at Gotha.

Though this programme said nothing about historical materialism of the theory of surplus value, it included the main principles on which Marx had insisted that any effective working-class party should be based. It recognised that the struggle of the workers against capitalism could not be confined to politics, as Lassalle had sought to do, or to economic reorganisation, as Proudhon believed, but had to be carried on in both spheres at the same time. It insisted that it was the task of the Social-Democratic Party to lead this struggle and to give the workers a consciousness of their mission to emancipate the whole of society by converting private property into social property and capitalist into socialist production. It declared, finally, that the class-struggle was not limited to the boundaries of a single nation, since all workers had common interests and that the party was, therefore, internationalist.

The programme then outlined the immediate demands of the party, such as the separation of Church and State, free education, medical services and legal facilities, progressive taxation, protective labour legislation, unrestricted rights of speech and assembly, and the full legal recognition of trade union organisations. After thirty years of intensive effort it seemed that the Marxists at last had the biggest working-class party in the world marching squarely behind them.

This Marxist victory, however, did not mean that the revolutionary wing of the party, which was convinced that peaceful reform alone would never break the strength of the capitalist system, had decisively routed the moderates, who sought to win power by constitutional methods. On the contrary, the rise of the Social-Democratic Party to a leading place in German politics only sharpened the conflict between the two sections. The main difference produced by the nominal conversion of the party to Marxist doctrine was that both wings of the party felt obliged to couch their arguments in Marxist terms, justifying their position by detailed and elaborate reference to the texts of the Marxist classics. Once the party had won a considerable number of seats in the Reichstag, many of its candidates receiving almost as much support from middle-class voters as from the workers, it had to decide whether it should accept its new role as a successful and comparatively respectable parliamentary body, or whether it should run the risk of further repression and of losing many of its more cautious supporters by holding to the spirit as well as the letter of Marxism. In the end the decision went in favour of the moderates, but the controversy was not easily settled.

The split between the two groups was quite obvious by the end of the 'nineties. For some time the socialists in Southern Germany, where industry was not so highly developed and political institutions were rather more democratic than in Prussia, had been criticising the party leadership for interpreting Marxism too literally. The party, they said, could only get the backing of the rural population if it stopped dogmatising about the inherent tendencies of capitalist society, and set about winning some immediate practical reforms.

This discontent, moreover, was not limited to one area. All through the party organisation there was a growing number of members who dismissed the traditional propositions of Marxism as inadequate and demanded that the party should revise the theoretical assumptions on which it was based. The bank clerk, Eduard Bernstein, who had become a party functionary and who had edited the illegal edition of the party organ from Zürich, became the chief spokesman of this group of 'revisionists', as they were called.

Bernstein left Germany in the year that the Anti-Socialist Laws were passed, spending the next twenty-two years in Switzerland and England before he returned home in 1900. For a time he had been a close associate of Engels and he was regarded as one of the most brilliant of the younger Marxists. But, as the years went on, he became more and more convinced that much of the Marxist analysis of capitalism was either wrong or obsolete. He was also an intimate friend of some of the leaders of the Fabian Society, and he was considerably influenced by their rejection of Marx and their belief in the gradual evolution of society towards a system of State socialism. He was, in fact, destined to play much the same role in Germany as they had in the British Labour Movement.

Eduard Bernstein began his attack upon the orthodox Marxists in a series of articles written for the party's theoretical paper, *Neue Zeit*, following these up with a long letter to a party conference that met in Stuttgart in 1898, and with his book *Evolutionary Socialism*, which appeared in 1899. Marx was wrong, Bernstein declared, in believing that the collapse of the capitalist system was imminent. Nor was he right in predicting that the gulf between the various classes in society would become wider and the class-struggle more bitter as the ownership of the means of production became concentrated in the hands of fewer and fewer people.

On the contrary, the development of the joint-stock company, in which ownership was dispersed among many thousands of shareholders, meant that there was 'an increasing number of capitalists of all degrees'. The middle-class was not disappearing but was becoming larger and more important. The advance of political democracy, the emergence of a State which was willing to recognise trade unions, to limit the exploitation of the worker by protective legislation, and to introduce a national system of social welfare and insurance, diminished both the need and the opportunity for the catastrophic change which Marx had anticipated.

There was, Bernstein insisted, no final aim of socialism: socialists should not display an excessive interest in some future society whose nature was unpredictable. 'The movement,' he said, in a famous phrase, 'is everything.' The party should concentrate its efforts on securing, one by one, the definite and limited reforms which, in aggregate, would gradually transfer control of society from a 'commercial land-holding oligarchy to a real democracy'. The labour theory of value, Bernstein argued, was little more than an abstract image. It was no use as a means of investigating the actual working of a capitalist economy. Similarly, Marx had produced a muddled and inadequate explanation of the periodic economic crises.

There was no evidence that, owing to the inability of capitalism to overcome its internal contradictions, these crises would become increasingly violent, culminating in a general collapse. Indeed, Bernstein believed that the enormous expansion of the wealth and trade of the main industrial countries, the elasticity of their credit system and the development of trusts and combines, had made capitalism more stable and that further great economic depressions were improbable. Socialists, consequently, had to look rather to the steady transformation of society by democratic methods than to the revolutionary tactics proposed by Marx in the days when the workers had no political rights and were confronted with a hostile State, dominated by the employers who exploited them. For the socialist movement was the heir to liberalism, with its regard for personal liberty, and it could not accept the thesis that the flexible liberal institutions of modern society should be overthrown and replaced by a dictatorship of the proletariat. That, Bernstein said, 'belongs to a lower civilisation, and apart from the expedience and practicability of the thing, it is only to be looked upon as a reversion'.

Thus, for Bernstein as for the Fabians, the State was not a class organisation. It was a partnership in which the workers had secured a considerable stake. They would accomplish all they desired through the intelligent use of their votes, without any real resistance from the capitalists, for 'the rights of the propertied minority have ceased to be a serious obstacle to social progress'.

With these arguments, elaborated continually throughout the next ten years, Bernstein provoked the most intense theoretical controversy, not only in the ranks of the Social-Democratic Party, but also among the socialist movements in other countries where Marxism had any influence. In this period, everything that Marx and Engels had either said or written was subjected to the closest scrutiny to prove that it was, or was not, applicable to the more highly-developed capitalist structure with which socialists had to reckon. It was, in fact, a dispute of critical importance in the history of socialism. (And for us, today. For the argument about the tactics of a minority movement at the end of the nineteenth century has become a quarrel between States, now that both communists and moderate socialists have become national governments, and now that the communists themselves have split on such issues between the 'revisionist' Russians and the 'militant' Chinese.) Was the movement in Europe to declare, as it had in England, that the revolutionary road to power was inappropriate in a democracy, that the capitalists would abdicate without a violent struggle, and that, in due course, by the steady accumulation of reforms, the socialist commonwealth would be achieved? Or was it to decide that the capitalist system could not afford concessions indefinitely, that it could not avoid relapsing into disastrous economic crises and, ultimately, into imperialist wars? If it accepted the first policy, it would certainly regard the revolutionary Marxists as greater enemies of progress than the capitalists. If, however, it heeded the warnings of the Left, it would prepare for a long and bitter fight for power, in which there would be no quarter from either side.

For the Left believed that if the advance of socialism within a capitalist democracy challenged the property rights of the ruling-class on a large scale, that class would be more ready to abolish the hard-won democratic rights of the workers than to give up its own wealth and privileges. Should the working-class pin its faith entirely on legal action and the possibility of change by general consent, it would find itself leaderless and impotent at the very moment when war or economic crises offered it the opportunity of winning power. By fostering the illusion that capitalism had changed its whole nature, especially since the development of the trusts, Bernstein and his associates, the Marxists said, were leading the movement to disaster.

But the Marxists themselves were by no means united. A few of them maintained an uncompromisingly revolutionary attitude and, as in the case of Rosa Luxemburg and the younger Liebknecht, later became the founders of the Spartacist League, the forerunner of the German Communist Party. Most of them followed the lead of Karl Kautsky, one of the most eminent Marxist theoreticians, who began as a strong opponent of Bernstein and later, in his hostility to communism, drifted into the company of the 'revisionists'.

Thus, in spite of its nominal commitment to Marxism, the Social-Democratic Party was split into warring factions. The Right wing of the party was quite open in its support for German imperialism, justifying it on much the same grounds as Shaw had endorsed the British war against the Boers and indulging at times in the most fervid eulogies of their country's civilising mission. The Centre had become so obsessed with practical reforms and philosophical abstractions that it had lost any realistic perspective of current developments, and almost to the outbreak of war in 1914 was asserting that there was no question of conflict because leading statesmen had assured the world that they desired peace. Though copious references were still made to Marx and to the traditions of the party, both these sections had become so involved in the politics of the German Empire that they had almost no idea at all where the Reich was heading.

Every time the radical elements in the party demanded that it should remember the traditional socialist opposition to militarism or should prepare itself for the impending war, they were denounced by both Right and Centre as extremists who were imperilling the striking progress the party had already made towards socialism. It was true that it was still the largest socialist movement in the world, with a vast organisation, a large number of newspapers and an impressive vote at elections. But it was a movement whose internal weaknesses were to be tragically exposed in the course of the war of 1914–18, and in the immediate post-war years.

In the conflict between the moderates and the revolutionaries the moderates had won, for very much the same reason as the Labour Party in England had passed under the leadership of the Fabians instead of the Social-Democratic Federation. German capitalism, like its English counterpart, passed through a period of expansion and prosperity, though the period was shorter and the prosperity not so great. It is characteristic of such periods that the socialist movement loses its militancy and endeavours to find a basis of compromise with the existing system.

Naturally, there were important differences between the Labour Party and the German Social-Democrats, not the least of which was the way in which the latter continued to repeat many of the traditional Marxist phrases long after they had ceased to have any relation with the practical policy of the Social-Democratic leaders. But Marxism was unimportant in England. The Labour movement inherited the tradition of radicalism from Bentham and J. S. Mill. Thus the Fabians found the ground already tilled for them when they set out to control the Labour Party. In Germany, however, as in a number of other countries in Europe, there was no other consistent socialist philosophy which had survived the impact of Marxism. Thus those who were really liberal reformers had to come forward as revisors of Marxism and not as its opponents. This paradox was one of the main reasons (the strength of nationalism was another) for the confusion that prevailed in the German Party at the approach and outbreak of the war in 1914.

THE FRENCH LABOUR MOVEMENT

The violent suppression of the Paris Commune in 1871 broke up the French working-class movement. Many of its leaders were shot in the streets of Paris, imprisoned or driven into exile. In the terror which followed the revolutionary outbreak it was virtually impossible to keep alive either the trade unions or socialist organisations. But the movement made a much quicker recovery from this setback than it had from the defeat of June 1848. Within a few years trade union activity began to revive again.

At first this took place under the leadership of the journalist Barbaret, who believed that trade unions would help to establish industrial peace, would act as educational centres and employment exchanges, and would eventually establish co-operative workshops as a means of eliminating extremes of wealth. By 1876 a large number of these unions had been organised—they were able to capitalise the support given by the French workers to the Proudhonist doctrine of consumers' and producers' co-operatives—and a central congress, attended by over four hundred delegates, was held in Paris. Barbaret must have been well satisfied with his efforts, for this congress went on record against strikes and affirmed the necessity of industrial harmony, refusing to take any notice of the handful of socialists who were present.

Nevertheless, Barbaret's success was comparatively shortlived. A nucleus of socialists—most of them old members of the International —had managed to survive through the difficult period after the

Commune. In 1877 they were joined by Jules Guesde, who had returned from exile in Switzerland, where he had been closely associated with the Marxist group. Guesde founded a new weekly paper,
L'Egalité, which from the start advocated the formation of a proletarian party aiming at the seizure of power and the creation of a
socialist society.

Thanks to the agitation carried on by Guesde and his associates,
and to the failure of the Proudhonist movement to do anything
very much to improve the condition of the workers, the idea of a
socialist party began to find increasing support. By the time the
third congress of syndicates met at Marseilles in 1879 the socialists
were in a majority. Guesde had been sent to prison in the previous
year for attempting to hold an international conference of workers
in Paris, and this, a resolution passed at Marseilles declared, had
shown that 'the working-class had no longer to expect its salvation
from anybody except itself'. It should, therefore, form its own
political party and struggle for the collective ownership of the land,
the factories and the utility services.

Once the enthusiasts for co-operation and conciliation had been
routed, however, the socialists began to differ among themselves.
First, there was an anarchist wing which denied that there was anything to be gained from parliamentary politics—which it denounced
as leading to corruption, compromise and absurdity—and insisted
that only a violent and conclusive insurrection could effectively
abolish the twin tyrannies of capitalism and the State. All other
forms of socialist activity, the anarchists declared, merely dissipated
the revolutionary ardour of the workers. Though it exercised more
indirect than direct influence, anarchism was sufficiently similar to
the doctrines of Proudhon, on which a whole generation of French
workers had been brought up, for it to secure a response among that
section of the working-class which still had no faith in normal
political measures. In 1883, for instance, after there had been a series
of disturbances in mining areas, sixty-six anarchists were put on
trial. One of them was Prince Peter Kropotkin, the Russian exile
who played a prominent part in the anarchist movement for more
than forty years, writing some of its finest historical and philosophical studies.

Apart from the anarchists, there were two other important groups which were divided more or less along the same lines as socialists in other countries. At the congress held in St. Etienne in 1882 the revolutionaries led by Jules Guesde had broken with the reformist wing, headed by Paul Brousse, the first section forming the French Workers' Party and the second adopting the name of the French Socialist Workers' Party.

Guesde had very little belief in the value of reforms. As long as capitalism lasted there was no guarantee that reforms were permanent or that they would not be withdrawn when it suited the ruling-class. Socialists should contest national and local elections because they offered an admirable opportunity for propaganda, not merely to win seats. As the constitution of the party declared, their role was to act as 'a kind of recruiting and instructing sergeant', preparing the masses for the seizure of political power in the inevitable crisis.

The Broussists, on the contrary, took much the same line as the Fabians in England and Bernstein in Germany. They believed that it was necessary to concentrate on electoral activity. Their representatives in the municipal or departmental councils, or in the Chamber of Deputies, were to secure the immediate reforms desired by the party by gaining the co-operation of other groups, either by persuasion or permeation. Unlike the revolutionary Marxists, who possessed a strongly-disciplined organisation, the reformists gave a good deal of latitude to their local sections and were prepared to admit all manner of persons to their party, provided that they subscribed to the most elementary socialist principles. This, however, did not prevent internal dissensions, and in 1890 a group of members, led by Allemane, broke away to form yet another party on the ground that the Broussists had paid too little attention to socialist agitation and too much to catching votes.

In addition to these four sections of the working-class movement there were two others which exercised some influence. The first—the Central Revolutionary Committee—consisted of former associates and supporters of the veteran conspirator August Blanqui. This group survived until 1904, in one form or another, but its younger members were gradually won over by the Marxists, and the old men, most of whom could not escape from the slogans which had carried them to the barricades in 1848 and 1871, lost touch with the changing feeling in the working-class movement. The second body, which emerged from a discussion circle in much the same way as the Fabian Society, was formed by a number of independent socialists who had become disillusioned with radicalism and turned to drafting schemes of social reform which, they hoped, would be widely endorsed. Some of these men, such as Millerand and Jean Jaurès, later played a prominent part in French politics.

The confusion created by the activity of so many organisations, each claiming that it alone had the insight or ability to lead the French workers, was naturally reflected in the syndicates, whose work was seriously hampered by factional disputes and by the existence of rivals in the same industry or district which owed allegiance to different parties. But as French industry and commerce developed, and the employers maintained their hostility towards all the unions, it became increasingly urgent to form a national federation of syndicates which could unite the workers in the industrial struggles. Though this federation was, in fact, set up at a congress in Lyons in 1886, it soon came under the leadership of the Marxists in the French Workers' Party. When this happened there was no hope of unity, for the other socialist groups refused to participate in the Federation once it had passed under Marxist control. They turned, therefore, to the creation of a parallel body, based on the labour exchanges (*Bourses du Travail*), which, legalised by the law of 1884, were springing up all over France.

Although these exchanges were founded with official assistance, they rapidly became much more than offices where workers could be hired. They acted as centres for local trade union activity, for meetings and for educational classes. Before long this new Federation of Labour Exchanges was dominated by the Allemanists, who, breaking away from the moderate Socialist Workers' Party, had taken with them some of the most able leaders of the syndicates.

The rival federations were scarcely launched when the old anarchist idea of a general strike began to gain support among the French workers. There were good reasons for this. The possibility of successful revolt in the traditional fashion, of which the anarchists and some of the Blanquists still dreamed, no longer seemed realistic. The prospect of victory through a long political struggle, as envisaged by the socialists, appeared distant and remote. The general strike was thus the sole weapon which the workers could use to emancipate themselves from capitalist exploitation.

In 1888 the Federation of Syndicates endorsed this view; three years later it was taken up by the Allemanists. The remnant of the Blanquists discovered that it fitted perfectly well into their programme. Only the Marxists objected to it. It was childish to imagine, they argued, that a peaceful general strike was possible. Revolutions could not be carried through under a pretence of legality. Even if the workers were willing to abstain from the use of force, there was no sign that the ruling-class would hesitate to suppress a movement which threatened to dispossess it. In any case, the interruption of vital services would bring starvation to the workers long before their employers went hungry. To undertake such an ambitious venture with any chance of success the workers would require to be so well organised and disciplined that they would have already reached the point where they could capture political power.

The Marxist refusal to accept the general strike led to an early breach between them and most of the syndicates. They were unable to stop the passage of a resolution favouring the strike at a conference of the Federation of Syndicates in 1892, and withdrew from it. From this date the Federation—which was changed into the General Confederation of Labour (the CGT) in 1895—declared its independence of all political parties and its support for an early general strike.

For the next few years the policies of the CGT and the Federation of Labour Exchanges ran on converging courses, and in 1903 a united CGT was formed which included them both. By this time, thanks partly to the efforts of Fernand Pelloutier, who was secretary of the Federation of Labour Exchanges until his death in 1901, there was widespread support for syndicalism, as the doctrine of revolution by direct industrial action alone was called.

The syndicalists had moved quite a long way in the direction of anarchism. They had discarded their earlier dislike of violence; they had even gone so far as to endorse sabotage; and they were convinced that the success of a general strike depended less on the resources and discipline of the workers than on the audacious leadership of a purposeful minority. They had also won over a substantial number of socialists who had become disillusioned with the policy of reform and class collaboration pursued by their leaders.

The drift towards syndicalism received a powerful impetus from the Millerand affair. In June 1899 Millerand agreed to enter the Radical Government of Waldeck-Rousseau, which was engaged in a struggle with the monarchist and clerical reaction—personified in the famous Dreyfus case—as Minister of Commerce and Industry. One of his colleagues was the notorious General Gallifet, who had been responsible for the slaughter of thousands of the Communards in 1871. The socialists, at this time, had more than fifty seats in the Chamber of Deputies. An important section, consisting for the most part of the moderate independent socialists and the Broussists, supported Millerand. Jean Jaurès even formulated a new theory for the occasion, arguing that capitalist society had entered a period of transition, in which the proletariat and the bourgeoisie could share power, and that the French socialists would thus be taking the logical course if they endorsed Millerand's decision to accept office.

But this thesis, which raised in an acute form the whole question of the socialist attitude towards reforms and parliamentary politics, was at once contested by the Marxists and the Blanquists, who, unfortunately for them, had no practical alternative to offer. Though the Marxists carried the dispute provoked by the 'treachery' of Millerand—and, later, of other socialists—into the international movement, in France at least they were themselves splitting into a reformist wing, which became preoccupied with electoral activity, and a revolutionary wing which drifted towards the syndicalists. The latter, in fact, crying a plague on all schools of socialism, were able to capitalise the resentment and impatience of workers who saw in the Millerand affair a final proof of the futility of dabbling in bourgeois politics.

The syndicalists accepted the Marxist doctrine that society was divided into two warring classes and that the workers were led inevitably to seek the destruction of the capitalist economy. They believed, however, that the syndicate, which united the workers on the basis of their common economic interests, was a far more stable unit of organisation than political parties, which, by making a political idea the sole link between men of different social origins and occupations, were liable to be disunited and ephemeral. The syndicate should be an industrial, rather than a craft, union, for this would strengthen the solidarity of the workers and assist in their mobilisation for strike action. The general strike, the instrument of social revolution, could not be called until the workers had been prepared for it in a series of strikes, in particular factories, in districts and in whole industries. These strikes would widen the gulf between the employers and the men by revealing the fundamental antagonism that existed between them and at the same time they would teach the workers valuable lessons in tactics and organisation.

Since the State was only the means through which the capitalist class exercised its authority—and here again the syndicalists took over a Marxist, or equally an anarchist, argument and adapted it to their own purposes—it should be treated in the same fashion. Such concessions as were necessary should be won by direct action, by street demonstrations. The syndicates should accept only those reforms which were won by force; all the rest were merely attempts to buy them off and should, therefore, be repudiated as liable to blunt the revolutionary temper of the workers.

Similarly, nationalism and militarism served to divide the working-class from its comrades in other lands who were engaged in the same struggle to emancipate themselves. The syndicalists were consequently pledged to oppose all preparations for war and the 'patriotic' propaganda that accompanied them. When the general strike was ultimately successful, all private property and class distinctions would be swept away, and the syndicates would then undertake the direction of production and distribution. While such services as the railways would be controlled by the CGT as the most suitable national co-ordinating body, local economic activity would be regulated by the appropriate Labour Exchange, representing all the syndicates in the district. Thus, for the first time, the workers would be drawn into the management of the enterprises in which they were employed. There would be no need for a political State once the necessity for a centralised authority and a means of class oppression had disappeared; such social discipline as would be required in a free and co-operative society would be exercised by the workers themselves.

The syndicalists never went much beyond this in their speculation about the future. They were averse to detailed plans, holding that their task was to change the system and leave the problem of what institutions were to replace it to those who actually had to create them. There was, however, one common point in their philosophy. They regarded majority rule as an illusion. Effective decisions, they said, could be taken only by an organised minority. If it had to submit its aims for the endorsement of the majority, it could not function efficiently. If the majority agreed, the vote was superfluous. If it disagreed, it was obstructing progress.

This principle applied to the work of the syndicates, which, under capitalism, could never hope to rally the entire working-class. They had, therefore, to act as a disinterested leadership and to accomplish, in the best interests of the whole of their class, the overthrow of the employers. The revolution could not wait until everyone realised that it was both desirable and necessary.

Apart from the syndicalists who were active leaders of the labour movement, there was also a small group of intellectuals which sought to construct a more sophisticated doctrine on the basis of the syndical agitation. Of these the most famous was Georges Sorel, who never had much direct influence on the French workers. Sorel insisted that the idea of a general strike was of great value in training and educating the workers for the destruction of capitalism. But it did not matter at all whether this strike ever occurred: it served as a myth to keep up the spirit of the workers in adversity, just as the myth of eternal life had sustained Christianity. Every great social movement, said Sorel, had its myth which served to concentrate its aspirations to the point of action. As long as the workers kept before them the millenial vision of the general strike, their enthusiasm for the fight against capitalism would be kept at fever pitch. This argument was accompanied by a good deal of abstract and mystical moralising.

Some of Sorel's doctrine, in a crude form, did indeed filter through to the syndicalist rank-and-file, but he himself became more and more reactionary. When, many years later, Mussolini came to set

down the rambling and obscure remarks that formed the political
testament of Italian fascism, he approvingly incorporated much that
he had learnt from Sorel. It was the catastrophic aspect of syndicalism that attracted Sorel. Men, he was convinced, did not become free
by changing their environment so much as by their dedication to
an heroic cause. They fulfilled themselves only when they substituted
moral and physical violence for the placid observance of social
conventions.

While the syndicalists were concentrating on their industrial
guerilla warfare against capitalism, the various socialist groups were
gradually drawing more closely together. In 1905, thanks in part to
the intervention of their comrades abroad and in part to the efforts
made by Jaurès to unite them, they formed the United Social Party.
In the next year it polled nearly 900,000 votes and returned fifty-one
deputies. Within eight years it had increased its vote to 1,400,000
and the number of its representatives in the Chamber to 103. Some
attempt was made to secure the affiliation of the CGT, but the
syndicates insisted on remaining free from all direct political
entanglements.

The Socialist Party itself, although it was nominally united, was
as much divided by dissenting elements as its counterpart in Germany.
The moderates, some of whose leaders had been expelled for following in the steps of Millerand, wanted to work with any party which
would introduce a few reforms in return for socialist votes in the
Chamber. The orthodox Marxists, though they had been converted
to constitutional action, still refused to accept such co-operation as a
matter of principle. The third group, led by Gustave Hervé, was
strongly influenced by the doctrine of the syndicalists. At the head
of the party stood Jaurès, who managed to hold the three groups
together in an uneasy alliance on a platform of social reform, anti-
militarism, State monopolies and—the reason for his assassination
at the outbreak of war—friendship rather than hostility towards the
German people.

When the war started, the breach between the socialists and the
syndicalists had not been healed, and the experiences of the war
years were to produce new and even more bitter divisions within
the labour movement. But although the syndicalists never staged

their general strike, and though they were slowly won over to less drastic methods, they made an important contribution to socialist theory. Like the Guild Socialists in England, on whom they exerted considerable influence, they called attention to the danger and inadequacy of a bureaucratic State socialism, and they revealed the potentialities of the trade unions, as both a weapon in the class-struggle and as the core round which the structure of a future economic democracy might be built—a doctrine that was paralleled by that of the Industrial Workers of the World in the USA. In their emphasis on the need for a militant minority to lead the working-class, and for the workers to be represented as producers rather than as citizens, they anticipated the communists' belief that their party should be a vanguard of devoted revolutionaries and that a hierarchy of soviets—or workers' councils—should replace a central parliament as the means of government.

12

LENIN AND THE BOLSHEVIKS

Throughout the nineteenth century, every liberal and democrat in Europe regarded Tsarist Russia as the bulwark of reaction: every autocrat considered the Tsar his natural ally, whose troops might be used to bolster up a tottering régime. There was widespread sympathy for the repeated but unsuccessful Polish revolts. To the West, Russia seemed a barbarous tyranny which stood on the fringe of civilisation. Until 1861 the serfs were still the personal property of their masters. After that date the free peasants were bled white by landlords and moneylenders; national and racial minorities were incited to persecute each other; there was no industrial development of any importance until nearly the end of the century; and a vast army of bureaucrats and spies was employed to secure obedience to the edicts of the Tsar and his attendant aristocracy. Criticism led to foreign exile. Siberia, or the gallows. There was scarcely any political or intellectual freedom.

In this backward and ramshackle empire, effective and organised opposition could be expected only from one source—the educated class. It is true that there were recurrent peasant disturbances, but these were mostly local and spontaneous, lacking any of the elements which could have transformed them into a general uprising except the desperate hatred of men who found their misery unbearable.

The intelligentsia, however, was strongly influenced by the ideas and events of Western Europe. The students, writers, poets and some of the younger officers had studied the literature and the philosophy of the West, especially of France and Germany. They could not fail to contrast the sordid and despotic system under which they lived with the liberties enjoyed in the world beyond the frontiers of Russia.

Some of them, like Bakunin and Kropotkin, became prominent figures in the international revolutionary movement. Those that remained in Russia were constantly persecuted by the police. For all their brilliance and their courage, they could accomplish little as long as they remained a tiny isolated group without mass support. After 1873, when the Tsar recalled hundreds of students from abroad, their was a brief period in which the intellectuals 'went to the people', living with them and trying to teach them the new ideas which they imported from the West. But this activity had not much success. The people found the greatest difficulty in understanding what these political missionaries were talking about. The Tsarist police, moreover, arrested thousands of them in an effort to stop their propaganda before it became really dangerous.

In the absence of any large-scale popular movement, which could be directed against the authorities, the Narodniks (literally 'Party of the People'), as the revolutionaries were called, fell back upon conspiracy and terrorism as the only means of securing the changes they desired. They were dominated by anarchist doctrine and translated Bakunin's belief in the value of violence into practice. A whole series of assassinations culminated in the murder of Tsar Alexander II in March 1881. But this act did not touch off a general rising. The Terrorists optimistically expected an insurrection, but they had done nothing to prepare one. On the contrary, it provoked a new campaign of repression against democrats and socialists of all kinds.

It was clear that sporadic violence was no more likely to break up the Tsarist régime than was peaceful propaganda. But most of the Narodniks had no idea what they should do next. They did not believe that society developed according to a definite pattern. History for them was made by the heroism of outstanding individuals and not by the struggle of classes. Capitalism, which had appeared in Russia by accident, had no future. It followed from this that the proletariat, which was still small and ill-organised, could be ignored by the intelligentsia and the peasantry, which were the only revolutionary elements that mattered. Socialism, the Narodniks were

convinced, would eventually be built on the traditional peasant commune. This position was understandable enough in a country where
a vast peasant population was held in control, for centuries, by a
bureaucracy wholly subservient to a central and absolute authority.
The Narodniks naturally believed that by eliminating the leading
figures of the régime the peasantry would gain their freedom. They
were aware, at least, of the immense difficulties that had to be faced
before socialism could be established in a nation of peasants
(difficulties that made Marx himself sceptical of the possibility of
successful revolution in Russia), and sought to avoid them by basing
socialism upon the peasant community rather than, as in Western
Europe, on the urban workers.

One section of the Narodnik movement, however, had realised
that this policy led into a blind alley, and it turned towards Marxism.
Under the leadership of Plekhanov the Marxists founded the Society
for the Emancipation of Labour in 1883. They were at once engaged
in a furious controversy with the remaining Narodniks. They
insisted that capitalism was already well established in Russia; that
the task of the revolutionaries was not to try to arrest its development but to provide a leadership for the growing working-class it
had produced; and that it was absurd to regard the peasant commune
—which was dominated by the wealthy farmers—as the embryonic
form of socialism. But though these early Marxists had a far better
understanding of the forces at work in Russia than the Narodniks,
they did very little practical work among the proletarians on whom
they staked their hopes. Their activity was almost entirely confined
to the organisation of study circles and they played no part in the
strike wave of the 'eighties.

Among the young revolutionaries who belonged to these Marxist
circles was Vladimir Ilyich Ulyanov, who adopted the pseudonym
of Lenin. He was born in the town of Simbirsk in 1870, the son of
a school inspector. His brother was hanged for complicity in a plot
to assassinate the Tsar and he himself had to leave Kazan University
for seditious activity. By the time Lenin arrived in St. Petersburg in
1893 he already had a close knowledge of Marxism, and two years
later he helped to unite all the Marxist groups in the city into a
League of Struggle. This body was the first in Russia to pass from

mere propaganda to agitation among the working-class, linking socialist philosophy to the immediate demands of the misery-ridden workers.

Although many members of the League were arrested, it succeeded in organising a number of important strikes and in stimulating the development of similar groups in many parts of Russia. But it was still impossible to weld these together into a single party. The congress which met at Minsk in 1898 for this purpose was attended by only nine delegates, who were arrested soon afterwards. The Russian Social-Democratic Labour Party had been founded in name only.

The Marxists made slow progress for the next few years. At the same time as they were striving to destroy the influence of the Narodniks, they had to fight against a new tendency that had appeared. This tendency, expressed by a group known as the 'Economists', was to insist that the workers should concentrate their efforts on the economic struggle with the employers and should leave political matters to the liberals and the democrats. The 'Economists', in fact, used virtually the same arguments against the formation of an independent party of workers as were used, with far more justification, in England. For although the English working-class had a great deal to gain by creating its own party, it was at least living under a constitutional government. The Russian proletariat, on the contrary, was denied even the most elementary rights and, as Lenin saw, it had nothing to lose by adopting illegal revolutionary methods.

But Lenin was in exile in Siberia and he could do little but plan for the future. It was during this period that he conceived the idea of starting a secret Marxist paper which, circulated on a large scale, would serve as a focus for the scattered Marxist groups, and as a major weapon in the ideological conflict with the Narodniks and the 'Economists'. As soon as he was permitted to return from Siberia, Lenin went abroad to arrange for the production of this paper, which was called *Iskra* (*The Spark*). The first issue was published in December 1900.

By this time there were nearly three million industrial workers in Russia, and though they were still a small fraction of the whole population, it was obvious that the Marxists had been right when they insisted that the proletariat would become the most militant and consistent revolutionary force in the country. In the first three years of the new century, which were marked by a serious crisis, hundreds of thousands of workers were involved in strikes.

In these strikes, which were mostly led by the Marxists, the workers put forward political as well as economic demands. The revolutionary movement was gaining ground, but there was still no organised party which could link these local strikes together or provide an effective leadership for the developing alliance of the proletariat and the peasantry against their common enemy the Tsarist régime.

Before such a party could be built there had to be some sort of agreement about its structure and the principles upon which it was to be based. In the columns of *Iskra*, and in his book *What Is To Be Done?*, Lenin insisted that the Russian Social-Democratic Labour Party could not be content to wait placidly until the workers spontaneously accepted socialist ideas. It had, on the contrary, to turn itself into a well-disciplined body of professional revolutionaries which would be capable of leading the proletariat steadfastly towards the conquest of power. Lenin did not want a party of reformists which would act as a parliamentary opposition once constitutional rights had been wrested from the Tsar. He believed that it was the mission of the Russian working-class to come forward as the champion of all the oppressed and exploited, to lead the peasants, the national and the racial minorities.

But Lenin's views were not shared by all those who wished to form a socialist party, in spite of the great influence exercised by *Iskra*. When, in 1903, a party congress was held in Brussels and then in London—really its inaugural congress, which, for reasons of safety, could not meet in Russia—the basic theoretical differences in the party found expression in a bitter dispute about its rules and programme. There were forty-three delegates present. Only twenty-four of them stood squarely behind Lenin. The remainder were vacillating moderates or else, like the three 'Economists' and the five representatives of the Jewish Bund, open opponents of the policy advocated by Lenin in *Iskra*.

Nevertheless, after a heated debate, Lenin succeeded in pushing through his draft of a party programme. This committed the social-democrats, on paper at least, to the struggle for: first, a democratic republic; and second, the dictatorship of the proletariat. But what mattered, as Lenin realised, was not the willingness of the delegates to accept a general statement of aims. The test of their sincerity to the cause of the revolution was the nature of the party they were prepared to create in order to win power. It was on this issue that the congress split.

Martov, one of the most prominent Russian Marxists, wished to admit anyone to the party who agreed with its aims, even if they were not willing to do active work for it. He wanted a loose demo-cratic organisation, open to any sympathiser, which would function in much the same way as the socialist parties of Western Europe. Lenin, however, insisted that party membership was a vocation; that the mark of a genuine revolutionary was his whole-hearted devotion to the party; and that, consequently, he should accept an iron discipline. Nothing else, he insisted, would ensure the survival of the party under conditions of terror and illegality, such as it faced in Russia, let alone its final victory in the turmoil of a revolution. In between congresses, which were the highest authority of the party, its members should follow the orders of the elected Central Com-mittee. In moments of crisis there would be neither time nor opportunity to undertake a consultation of the whole membership after the fashion of legal parties in the West. If Martov's proposal was adopted, the party would be opened to all sorts of rabble who could contribute nothing but confusion and who might actually destroy it. When the issue came to a vote, Lenin was defeated. But this defeat did not settle the matter, as the 'Economists' and the members of the Bund withdrew from the congress after a dispute on another issue. This tipped the balance in Lenin's favour once more. In the vote for the Central Committee and for the editorial board of *Iskra* Lenin's supporters were elected. It was from the voting on these two questions that the two rival sections of the party took the names by which they have since been called. The majority, from the Russian word *bolshinstvo*, were known as the Bolsheviks. Martov's group, the minority, became the Mensheviks.

The voting at the London congress was too close to settle the dispute one way or the other, and once the split had taken place on this formal issue the two sections of the party found themselves at loggerheads on a number of fundamental questions. The Bolsheviks were unable to maintain the advantage they had secured in London. By winning over a few key individuals, particularly Plekhanov, the Mensheviks secured control both of *Iskra* and of the Central Committee. The Bolsheviks thereupon issued a new paper and set up a central body to organise their own supporters. Thus, on the eve of the Russian revolution of 1905 there were two distinct groups, nominally united, but each possessing its own organisation and policy, and each claiming that it alone should act as the leadership of the working-class.

Nobody planned the revolution of 1905. It was the outcome of the disastrous defeats in the Russo-Japanese war, coming as they did on top of a serious economic depression. Popular indignation with the incompetent conduct of the war and with the frightful casualties suffered by the Russian armies coincided with a new wave of strikes, many of them led by the Bolsheviks. On January 9th, 1905, a vast procession of workers marched to the Winter Palace in St. Petersburg to present a petition to the Tsar. They demanded freedom of speech and organisation, the convocation of a constituent assembly, division of Church and State, the grant of land to the peasants and peace with Japan. Nicholas II answered their requests by ordering the police and troops to open fire. At least one thousand workers were shot.

This massacre was the signal for disturbances all over Russia. In January alone more than five hundred thousand workers went on strike. For several months there were strikes, riots and street fighting in the big towns. The peasants rose in one district after another, burning the houses and seizing the land of their masters. In June the sailors on the battleship *Potemkin* mutinied and sailed away to Rumania. The revolutionary movement was spreading rapidly.

But what sort of revolution was it? The Mensheviks and the Bolsheviks had different answers to this question when each group held its own congress early in 1905. It was, said the Mensheviks, a liberal-democratic revolution and should, therefore, be led by the liberals and the democrats and not by the workers. It was necessary for the proletariat to act with restraint and to refrain from extreme demands in case it frightened the middle-class away from the revolution altogether. Socialism was not immediately possible in Russia, since the country was backward economically. The workers, therefore, should not take part in any provisional government that might be formed and should leave the task of drafting a constitution to the liberal parties. The Bolsheviks, however, were not prepared to accommodate their tactics to the timidity of their liberal allies. These, the Bolsheviks argued, were only interested in winning limited concessions and were much more afraid of the workers and peasants than of the Tsarist régime. It was the duty of the working-class to push the revolution as far as it could, because it required the conditions of political democracy in order to complete its preparations for the next stage of the struggle.

Lenin, in fact, had already worked out the essential features of the strategy that was to carry the Bolsheviks to victory only a few years later. He did not accept the Menshevik view that it was necessary for Russia to pass through a fairly long period of industrial capitalist development, at the end of which the workers would somehow seize power. He believed that, for a number of reasons, it was possible in Russia to go straight on from the bourgeois to the proletarian revolution without any need for a pause. It was thus necessary for the working-class to isolate the liberals and to assume the leadership of the movement as quickly as it could. Moreover, unlike the socialists of the West, who regarded the peasants as an obstacle to progress, Lenin realised that they were the natural allies of the proletariat and that the conquest of power was impossible without their co-operation. He therefore sought to forge a close alliance between the two classes which would fight against the Tsarist Government and neutralise the liberals. Owing to the late and distorted development of capitalism in Russia, the struggle against autocracy and the struggle for socialism had overlapped.

While the socialists were deciding what attitude they should adopt towards the revolution, it was spreading with increasing speed. In October a huge strike occurred, involving more than a million industrial workers, apart from the employees of the railway and the postal services. It was in the course of this strike that the soviets (or councils of workers) made their first appearance. They were formed by delegates elected directly from factories and other enterprises and acted, for a short time, as the effective authority in the towns where they were set up, introducing freedom of the Press and, in some cases, confiscating State taxes for their own revolutionary purposes. The strike wrung promises of reform from the Tsar, including a general franchise and a legislative assembly.

These concessions, the Bolsheviks said, showed that the old régime was unable to govern any longer by the old methods. But they were not enough. A final armed uprising was necessary to overthrow the tottering system. The revolt started in Moscow in December 1905. It was accompanied by strikes and uprisings from Finland to the Ukraine and Georgia. But the Tsarist Government was still strong enough to suppress the scattered insurrection, and thousands of revolutionaries were killed in the fighting, or executed, or thrown into prison. For months, punitive expeditions scoured Poland, Siberia, Transcaucasia and the Baltic provinces. The revolutionary tide had turned. There were a number of revolts in the years after 1906, but the chance had been lost once the opposition parties, apart from the Bolsheviks, had refused to resort to arms and had left the revolutionaries to their fate.

Though the Tsar kept his promise and convened a Duma, or legislative assembly, its powers were limited and its life was short. As soon as it began to make definite demands it was forcibly dissolved. Its successor suffered the same fate. The electoral law was then revised in order to increase the number of representatives who supported the Tsar, one deputy being elected by every two hundred nobles and one by every hundred thousand workers. This new Duma sat throughout the period of reaction that lasted until 1912. It tolerated the imprisonment of no less than two hundred members of the First Duma and the Second Duma—in which the revolutionaries had not even participated—the execution of thousands and the banishment of about two hundred thousand people to Siberia.

Inside the socialist movement, which found it difficult to keep going at all under this reign of terror, there was still a bitter theoretical struggle between the two rival sections. The Mensheviks were demanding that there should be no illegal revolutionary work on the grounds that this was endangering the whole existence of the party. They wanted to confine their activity to socialist education and to such methods as were still tolerated. The Bolsheviks, however, insisted that the party should go on steadily preparing for insurrection so that the opportunity would not be lost a second time. In spite of the severe difficulties under which they had to work, they managed to hold their supporters together. Finally, at the congress of the social-democrats in Prague, in 1912, they formally expelled the Mensheviks and Lenin at last had his united and disciplined party of professional revolutionaries.

From 1912 onwards the revolutionary revival began to resemble the course of events that had preceded the outbreak of 1905. The shooting of five hundred strikers in the Lena goldfields in Siberia touched off a new series of mass strikes and political demonstrations. All over Russia, under Bolshevik leadership, there was unrest among the workers, peasants and the armed forces. But this time the strikers were demanding a new revolution, not reforms. The Bolsheviks were still outnumbered by the other opposition parties, which ranged from the Mensheviks on the Left to the peasant Social-Revolutionaries and the Constitutional Democrats on the Right. But they were the most militant and best-organised of them all. The Russian socialist movement was no more united than its counterparts in the West, but in Russia it was at least clear which groups stood for the constitutional reform and which for revolution on the Marxist model.

The outbreak of the war threw the European socialists into confusion. Most of the parties supported it from the start and only later began to consider whether they could do anything to bring it to an end. In Russia the Bolsheviks realised that it would mean a temporary setback until the masses learnt through their own suffering that the war was nothing more than an imperialist conflict. Then, they believed, their chance would come and they would be able to bring the uneasy partnership between capitalism and the autocracy tumbling down in ruins. It was an omen that there were barricades on the streets of St. Petersburg at the moment war was being declared.

E

13

THE SECOND INTERNATIONAL AND THE WAR

By the outbreak of the World War in 1914 socialism had become a considerable force in European politics. The most striking progress had been made, as we have seen, in France and Germany, where there were large working-class parties which counted their supporters by the hundred thousand. But all over the Continent socialist organisations of some kind had been set up and had begun to play a part in the affairs of their respective countries. There were parties even in Argentina and the United States, where Eugene Debs, the socialist candidate for the Presidency, polled nearly 900,000 votes in the elections of 1912.

Though all these movements had adapted themselves with some success to the specific national conditions under which they had to work, this did not mean that the idea of international action had been forgotten. On the contrary, a new body had been formed to take the place of the old First International and to co-ordinate, as far as possible, the policies and work of its affiliated parties. Most of these were strongly influenced by Marxism and, nominally at least, were committed to the doctrine of the unity of the workers of all lands against capitalism and against war. But, as the World War was to reveal, this sense of unity was not strong enough to hold the movement together once the workers were called upon to defend their native land. Nationalism then took precedence over socialism.

The Belgian socialist leader, Emile Vandervelde, once described the First International as a brilliant general staff without an army.

Its successor, however, possessed an army of millions but lacked an effective general staff. From its birth as an organised centre in 1901 —though there had been occasional congresses before this—until it disintegrated in 1914, the Second International never had any real power to control the parties which belonged to it. Since it was open to any group which accepted the broad principles of socialism, regardless of the doctrine on which it was based, it served primarily as a forum in which questions of general and theoretical interest were discussed. From time to time it did intervene in the activities of the socialists in particular countries—in France, for instance, it was instrumental in unifying the rival parties in 1905—but, even if it had wished to do so, it could not have issued orders and received unquestioning obedience from so large and so loose an organisation.

It is true that the decisions of its successive congresses were sometimes accepted by individuals or by parties which disagreed with them, but this secured formal rather than real agreement. The size of the International was a deceptive measure of its strength. It was little more than a numerical aggregate of its constituent parties. As such its proceedings reflected the theoretical and practical differences which divided these parties themselves. The struggle between the reformists and the revolutionaries to take the most fundamental issue, was fought out as bitterly at the congresses of the International as within the ranks of the various national parties.

But, in a period of comparative peace, when socialists appeared to be making steady progress everywhere, this structural weakness did not seem to matter very much. The leaders of the Second International proved to their own satisfaction that as long as they continued to act as a central clearing-house, publishing detailed and valuable reports on the activities of the various parties and on social problems of general concern, they were doing virtually all that was required of them.

Numbers, for them, were the important thing. As good parliamentary politicians, they measured their success in terms of the votes they commanded and not, as did Lenin and the other radical Marxists, by the discipline and unity of their supporters. In the same way they were well satisfied with the International because it had affiliated sections all the way from Portugal to Armenia and Norway to Bulgaria. Nothing, they felt, could now frustrate the advance of this invincible army. Each year brought it closer to victory. Even in distant Australia there had been a minority Labour Government—the first in the world—in 1904, while in nearby New Zealand the Labour Party was sufficiently strong to take part in a coalition with the Liberals before the nineteenth century reached its end. Socialism, it was true, was still a minority movement, but only time was needed to remedy that.

This attitude, we can see today, was based on an illusion, but it accounts for the extraordinary contrast between the apparent strength and unity of the Second International and its collapse almost overnight in the summer of 1914. It had devoted a good deal of time to debating the attitude of socialists towards war. In 1907, at a congress in Stuttgart, a famous resolution was carried which urged the workers to do everything in their power to prevent a conflict. If they were unable to do this, they were to try to bring it quickly to an end and to use the resulting economic and political crisis to rouse the people and thus hasten the downfall of capitalism. At the Copenhagen Congress in 1910 another resolution instructed socialist representatives to vote against the war credits of their respective governments.

Two years later, at Basle, more than five hundred delegates supported a motion declaring that it was a crime for workers of various countries to shoot one another for the sake of increasing the profits of the capitalists. There was, it would seem, very little doubt about the question. The policy had been thrashed out openly and a majority of the socialist parties had endorsed it. But if they had taken the resolutions seriously they would have begun to prepare for a hard revolutionary struggle. It was typical of most of the parties belonging to the Second International that they did nothing of the kind, although they were perfectly willing to accept, in theory, decisions which could not mean anything else.

In the last weeks of July 1914, when it was clear that war was imminent, attempts were made to implement the policy to which the Second International was committed. But it was then too late. On the 29th of July, while the leaders of the European socialist parties were meeting in Paris to consider how they could prevent the war, the powerful Austrian party had already decided to support the attack on Serbia. Müller, one of the German representatives, who announced that his party would not under any circumstances vote for war credits, returned to Berlin just in time to join his comrades in voting for the first credit of ten milliard marks. In France, Jean Jaurès was assassinated two days after he had called for opposition to the war, and on the day he was buried the socialists in the Chamber unanimously decided to enter the Government until Imperial Germany was crushed. The same story was true of Belgium.

The British Labour Party, though a section of the party, including Hardie and MacDonald, was anti-war, decided to give conditional support for the Liberal Government's decision to fight. Only the tiny party in Serbia and the Russian Bolsheviks took their stand on the Stuttgart and Basle resolutions. The Second International was in ruins.

There was, however, a minority in each of the larger parties which opposed the war and denounced the majority sections for betraying the fundamental socialist principles of internationalism and anti-militarism. In some cases, like the ILP in England, this minority was pacifist rather than revolutionary, but in general the division followed much the same lines as the pre-war cleavage between the reformists and orthodox Marxists. These groups managed to hold an international conference at Zimmerwald in 1915. Apart from Lenin and the other Bolsheviks living in exile in Switzerland, all the thirty-three delegates represented countries that were either neutral or fighting on the side of Germany. At this conference, and at its successor held in the village of Kienthal a year later, manifestos were drafted denouncing the war as the outcome of imperialism and capitalist rivalry, and urging the immediate conclusion of peace without annexations or indemnities. But at neither conference did the Bolsheviks succeed in winning a majority for Lenin's thesis that socialists should seek to turn the imperialist war into a civil war, should work for the defeat and overthrow of their own governments, and should decisively break with the moderates and reformists who supported the war, forming a new and revolutionary Third International.

These proposals seemed too drastic at a time when there was still no widespread opposition to the war among the workers of the belligerent nations and when the major Powers seemed capable of continuing the war indefinitely.

But the deadlock was broken more quickly than anyone expected. By the beginning of 1917 Russia was exhausted. The Tsarist régime was unable to suppress the discontent in the defeated and decimated armies or in the big towns. The Empire of Nicholas II was falling to pieces and there was nobody able or willing to hold it together. In March the troops who were called out to put down a mass political strike in Petrograd refused to obey orders, and joined the workers in the streets. Within two days the struggle was over in Petrograd, and the revolution had spread throughout Russia and to the armies at the front. Hungry, disillusioned and miserable, the subjects of the Tsarist régime had risen and destroyed it.

But what had taken its place? Everyone, from the liberals to the Bolsheviks, agreed that the March victory had at last completed the democratic revolution which began in 1905. Autocracy had been overthrown, and it seemed to liberal observers that Russia might gradually develop along the same lines as the countries of the West.

The Provisional Government, which had been set up by the Fourth Duma, promised to convene a constituent assembly to draft a new political structure and to carry on the war at the side of the Allies. In this it was supported by a majority in the Workers' and Soldiers' Soviets, which had sprung up rapidly and which were, at this time, under the leadership of the Mensheviks and the Social-Revolutionaries. But the Bolsheviks alone insisted that the revolution which started in March must be continued until the Provisional Government, dominated by representatives of big business and Russia's small middle-class, had itself been replaced by an alliance of peasants and workers. The collapse of the Tsarist régime, the Bolsheviks argued, did not automatically change the war from an imperialist to a progressive conflict.

Soon after the first revolution Lenin returned to Russia from Switzerland. He found that his own party was divided about the war. In fact, most of his adherents who met him at the station on the April night that he arrived in Petrograd (Leningrad today) were startled by the violence with which he denounced any attempt to continue the war as merely a continuation, by pseudo-revolutionaries, of the aggressive purposes of the Russian bourgeoisie. Lenin had to fight hard against even his closest friends and adherents in order to swing the Bolsheviks wholeheartedly behind his policy of 'revolutionary defeatism'. The Russian people, he argued, had nothing to gain from continued participation in the struggle. Alexander Kerensky, the dominant figure in the succession of provisional governments that held power precariously through the summer of 1917, might insist that the war had become a war of defence in which the Russians sought no more than the protection of their frontiers and the fulfilment of their commitments to the Allies. As far as Lenin was concerned, Kerensky insisted in vain. The more lives that were squandered in futile offensives, the more the Bolsheviks raised the cry of peace at any price. As long as Russia continued to associate with the Allies, the war remained imperialist and it was the duty of a revolutionary to stimulate disaffection and unrest and to work— whether he was a German or a Russian, Lenin reiterated—for the defeat of his own government.

If it was difficult for Lenin to carry his own party with him, it was equally hard for the Bolsheviks to escape the charge of treachery. Tardy repression, indeed, did drive the party underground as the summer wore on, but too late to save the Kerensky régime. For Russia was disintegrating under the blows of the German army, under the pressure of military mutiny, of peasants hungry for land and peace, of insurgent and ill-fed urban workers, and of the national minorities for whom, in Lenin's phrase, Russia was a 'prison-house'. The Bolsheviks, few though they were at this time, were able to exploit every tension to their advantage. The more their opponents rallied round the increasingly inept and unpopular Provisional Government, the better the Bolsheviks could isolate them from a people which was war-weary and hungry. The peasants, Lenin said, 'voted with their feet'. They would fight no longer—and the Bolsheviks, as the peace party, reaped the benefits of their anger and exhaustion.

Lenin, of course, was running enormous risks by this policy. It was one thing to call for peace as a revolutionary tactic against a war government: it was a different matter when the revolution itself might be endangered by total defeat at the hands of the German army. Yet Lenin counted on revolution inside Germany coming to the aid of Russia and, in any case, he believed that if the Bolsheviks supported the war they would lose the chief attraction their policy possessed: the desire for peace. Support of the war would have meant the end of Bolshevik hopes for a further revolution that would put them in power. Lenin knew this, and knew also that if he missed this chance to push through the seizure of power in 1917 it might not occur again for a long time. The times were ripe. Whatever the hazards, the Bolsheviks had to push on. A Bolshevik march was broken up by troops in July. This disheartened some of Lenin's comrades, but merely increased his determination to succeed. From the hiding-place to which he had fled from Kerensky's police, just across the Finnish border, Lenin directed a stream of letters and pamphlets at the Bolshevik Central Committee, denouncing those who drew back from another uprising as traitors, weaklings and incompetents.

At last, early in November (October 24th by the Russian calendar), plans were complete, though at the last minute such leading Bolsheviks as Zinoviev and Kamenev objected that the revolt was a wild and doomed folly. Lenin knew what he wanted. He had bullied and cajoled his party into the desperate attempt. On November 7th insurgent groups seized Petrograd after a very short struggle. Moscow fell soon after. The Provisional Government was dissolved and the Bolsheviks, with some allies from the Left of the other parties, proclaimed themselves the rulers of Russia. Lenin, in the face of apparently insuperable obstacles, had carried through his proletarian revolution. He had never believed that socialism could be achieved by electoral successes, least of all in Russia, where even free speech and assembly had been wanting until the overthrow of the Tsarist régime. Defeat in war had given him his chance, and when, as he said, 'power fell into our hands like a ripe fruit', he made sure that he had armed force enough to hold it.

All the other parties, from the Mensheviks to the liberals, denounced the revolt as treachery and tyranny, but they could do little about it. Their day was over. They had to choose between support of the Bolshevik régime and the counter-revolution. In Russia, at least, the dispute about the methods the workers should adopt to win power was no longer a theoretical issue. It had been settled in the streets of Petrograd in favour of the Marxist revolutionaries. While the reformists debated, the Bolsheviks had armed. For more than ten years Lenin had insisted that Russia would be able to pass straight from the bourgeois to the proletarian revolution. When the troops of the Revolutionary Military Committee, led by Leon Trotsky, established the first communist government in the world, they brought to pass the Marxist prophecy in the one country of which the Marxists, from Marx himself to Lenin, had previously had least hope. Russia, as Lenin said that evening, would proceed to the inauguration of socialism.

This, however, was no easy task. The peasants had quickly taken the land they desired. But there was widespread hunger; the resources of the country had been squandered in the war; industry was almost at a standstill; there was chaos everywhere and in everything. Yet the peace Lenin had demanded could not be secured as easily as the estates of landlords. Germany would not easily relinquish her hopes of vast plunder from a defeated Russia nor her demands for territorial satisfaction, especially in the Ukraine. While the negotiations dragged on at Brest-Litovsk the Bolsheviks found themselves forced to continue a fighting retreat. At times, when the German terms seemed outrageous, Lenin was in a minority on the Bolshevik Central Committee, most of whose members—including Trotsky—preferred to fight on rather than accept an intolerable peace. But Lenin was adamant. Any terms short of the actual destruction of the Bolshevik régime had to be accepted, to give the new state a breathing-space, in which it could be both consolidated and rehabilitated.

Eventually the Bolsheviks signed a peace treaty with Germany at Brest-Litovsk. While this treaty awarded the Germans a large part of Russia—it was all to be recovered after the German collapse—and permitted them to move a large part of their troops away from the Russian front to Western Europe, it is unlikely that the Bolshevik régime would have survived but for the chance this temporary peace gave it to consolidate. For within a few months, counter-revolution, aided by the Germans and by the Allies, had broken out in various parts of Russia. The remnants of the Tsarist army, joined both by

wealthy landlords and merchants as well as opponents of Bolshevism ranging as far to the Left as Social Revolutionaries and Mensheviks, were in arms against the young Soviet Republic, holding
huge areas of the country. They imposed a 'White Terror', backed
by foreign troops, arms and money, to which the Bolsheviks reacted
in turn. The Civil War merged into the War of Intervention—the
memory of which still lingers in Russia today as a barrier to friendly
relations with the outside world.

At one time the Bolsheviks held only a comparatively small part
of Russia around Petrograd and Moscow. It seemed that the Bolsheviks would inevitably be crushed. They were not. Their iron
discipline held the régime together: if they won there was the chance
of building a new society. If they lost, as many people who had little
sympathy with their more extreme proposals realised, Russia would
drift rapidly into ruin and the old aristocrats and landlords would
come back behind the White armies and the troops of the capitalist
Powers who were fighting against the Bolsheviks. Better the uncertain though rosy future promised by the Marxists than a return
to the old misery. It was this combination of hope and desperation
that rallied the people of Russia and the former oppressed nations
and sustained the improvised Red Army in its struggle on seventeen
different fronts simultaneously. For a time the Bolsheviks introduced
a system of military communism, in which every aspect of life was
subordinated to the central authority in the effort to survive.

After the war against the Whites and the Allied armies of intervention had been won, Russia needed a breathing-space to restore
the dreadful losses of the past seven years. The Bolsheviks then,
under the New Economic Policy, relaxed some of the restrictions on
small business and on private farming, though they still kept the
large industries under State ownership and control.

During the war years, however, all this lay in the future. Very few
people in Russia, let alone in the outside world, had any idea of the
course events were to take. The Bolsheviks appeared in the West as
a handful of desperadoes, probably subsidised by the Germans, who
had taken Russia out of the war and—what seemed far more
dangerous—had expropriated the capitalists and landlords according
to the traditional Marxist programme. These fears were encouraged

by the constant appeals that the Bolsheviks made to the workers of the Powers that were still at war, urging them to follow the Russian example, to overthrow their rulers and to make a just peace.

In these years Lenin was convinced that the revolution would spread. He regarded the victory in Russia as merely the prelude to the bigger and more bitter struggle that would come in the more advanced industrial countries. Russia was the base for this inevitable conflict. The links which held the capitalist world together had been broken at their weakest point. Soon, he believed, the workers of the world would finally unite for the last fight of which they had sung so often in the *Internationale*. Though there was little contact between the rest of Europe and blockaded Russia, enough was known of the revolution for the workers elsewhere to realise that, in some way, their comrades were the masters of a great country, that there was a practical way of ending the suffering caused by the war and, at the same time, of winning power for themselves.

The revolutionary groups which had all along opposed the war naturally acclaimed the Bolshevik victory. But it also evoked a response even from the moderates, who were increasingly uneasy about a war they had once, in every country, enthusiastically supported. Though they disliked the methods of the Bolsheviks and were not at all anxious to be involved in similar activities themselves they could not acquiesce in the destruction of the first successful socialist revolution.

Lenin regarded this foreign sympathy as one of the chief assets of the Bolsheviks. To co-ordinate it, and to provide a rallying-point for the growing revolutionary movement, he and the Bolsheviks formed the Third International. This, unlike its predecessor, was intended to act as a general staff for the proletariat of the world. It was to be highly disciplined; all its member parties were to base themselves uncompromisingly on the Leninist interpretation of Marxism; and it was to admit only those groups and individuals who had cut themselves off from the old reformist parties which, Lenin insisted, had disgraced themselves by supporting an imperialist war.

In vitriolic language the Bolsheviks denounced the moderates for leading the working-class into an impasse. They had encouraged illusions about peaceful change; they had betrayed the workers who had trusted them by entering into disgraceful alliances with their own capitalists against their fellow workers in other countries; and finally, when the supreme opportunity had arrived, they were too comfortable and too timid to seize it. Did they want socialism or not? Did they imagine that the greatest social change in history could be accomplished by agreement with the very class that had to be overthrown? The war was not a terrible accident. It was the inevitable product of imperialist rivalries. Unless the capitalist system were liquidated there would be a whole series of such world wars, each succeeded by a more calamitous economic crisis. Certainly, bloodshed would be necessary to establish socialism. But the cost would be small compared with the suffering and destruction that would follow if capitalism were allowed to continue. The working-class movement must not shirk its responsibilities now that the old society had begun to disintegrate.

The Bolshevik appeals began to yield results. In France an important section of the Socialist Party had begun to vote systematically against war measures, to demand a compromise peace and support for the Russian Revolution. Army mutinies were accompanied by strikes in the factories.

The same was true, though on a larger scale, in Germany, where the most extreme elements in the Social-Democratic Party had moved almost to the Bolshevik position. Even in England there was widespread industrial unrest, particularly on the 'Red' Clyde, and even before the Bolshevik revolt, though after the first (February) Revolution a completely futile attempt had been made to form a national network of councils on the soviet model. In every belligerent country there was a profound weariness and growing opposition to a continuation of the war. By the end of 1917 the revolutionaries were no longer an isolated sect.

Throughout the late summer of 1918 Germany was rapidly approaching the end of its resources. Apart from the workers, a large part of the peasantry and sections of the middle-class were demanding peace. The Government was unable to check the great strikes in the munition industries called by the extreme Left. The Social-Democratic leaders, however, still regarded it as their duty to fight on, though they made continued support of the war conditional upon the immediate introduction of certain reforms and the conclusion of a peace which restored the independence of Belgium and the territories filched from Russia by the onerous treaty signed with the Bolsheviks at Brest-Litovsk.

But, by November, nothing could save Germany. The Allies had broken Hindenburg's army. The soldiers and sailors were mutinying. Even before an armistice could be secured and the Kaiser driven to abdicate, the Revolution had started and the troops had begun to join the workers in the streets of Berlin, and other centres. For two or three days it seemed that the extreme Left might win control. But the moderate socialists had no intention of permitting an upheaval on the Russian model. They quickly put themselves at the head of the Revolution and sought to limit its scope. Ebert, their leader, was even reluctant to proclaim the end of the monarchy, but his colleague, Phillip Scheidemann, fearing that Karl Liebknecht and the revolutionary Marxists were about to call for a communist republic, forestalled them by announcing the substitution of a democratic republic for the dynasty. He did this on his own initiative, much to the fury of Ebert, who had been negotiating for the formation of a constitutional monarchy with one of the Kaiser's younger sons at its head.

From the first the moderates showed that they were more terrified of the Left than of the Right. In a considerable part of Germany local power was in the hands of revolutionary soviets. The communist groups and the bigger Independent Socialist Party, which had carried the non-Bolshevik but radical elements out of the main social-democratic organisation, were demanding that the revolution be continued until the power of the ruling-class had been broken.

This was the last thing that the moderates wanted, for they could see themselves being swept away just as Kerensky had been pushed aside in Russia. If Germany fell into the hands of the communists, they believed, the Allies would occupy the whole country and dictate a ruinous peace. Germany, in any case, was not yet ripe for socialism: the huge vote they now commanded was not a vote for the expropriation of the capitalists but merely for social reforms. All that could be done, without disorganising the whole economy of the country, was to limit the activities of monopolies and to establish a democratic capitalist State.

Some changes, of course, were necessary, but civil war, starvation and chaos would be unavoidable if order were not immediately restored and the reactionary parties were not reconciled to the gains that the revolution had already achieved. These arguments, naturally, did nothing but infuriate many of the workers. They saw the social-democratic leaders acting exactly as the Bolsheviks had predicted they would act, as the allies and defenders of capitalism at a moment when it appeared to be on the verge of collapse. Strikes, demonstrations and even street fighting followed.

Ebert, now President, had to fall back on the conservatives and the militarists for support. In fact, he actually made a secret alliance with Field-Marshal Hindenburg for common action against the communists. Hundreds of ex-officers, the forerunners of the Nazi storm troops, were mobilised into formations which could be used to suppress the revolutionary movement. In 1919 one of these squads murdered both Karl Liebknecht and Rosa Luxemburg. Fearing a communist success, the moderates turned for support to the people who most hated both German democracy and German socialism. They did nothing to break the power of the Junkers or of the huge capitalist trusts. They split the working-class into two irreconcilable sections—a breach that was never healed and undoubtedly paved the way for the Nazi victory in 1933.

Yet the communists were no less to blame. Following a sectarian policy (and rent by factional disputes that reflected the factionalism of the Soviet leadership), they waged a bitter campaign against the socialists; while they were also opposed to the Nazis, their policies helped make stable government impossible, and contributed to the growing totalitarian trends in Germany. For a crucial period, they even believed that Hitlerism would be a short-lived phenomenon, and that a temporary triumph for the Nazis would drive the whole working-class movement into the communist camp—and that a successful workers' revolution would follow. It was a disastrous error.

Elsewhere in Europe, the war had ended in revolutionary out-breaks. The Austro-Hungarian Empire had disintegrated and its component nationalities had set up their own States. In Austria itself there was an abortive communist revolt, while Hungary, for a short time, became a Soviet Republic, led by Bela Kun. But this régime was soon suppressed by the Rumanian armies, backed by the victorious Allies. Though Poland had at last won independence, it had been drawn into the war against the Bolsheviks and had suppressed the revolutionary movement. Nowhere outside Russia, however, did the communists manage to repeat the Bolshevik success. By 1920 Lenin realised that the tide had turned and that there was no immediate possibility of an extension of the proletarian revolution to the West.

But, in spite of the failure of the European workers to follow the Russian example, the Bolsheviks were by no means isolated. The Communist International, with its headquarters in Moscow, was growing in importance as, in one country after another, disciplined parties consciously based on the Bolshevik model were formed by the revolutionaries. In Europe alone they claimed a membership of more than one million. One or two of the old socialist parties had affiliated to the Comintern as a whole; elsewhere a large section had broken away to set up a new communist organisation. Communism, whatever setbacks it might temporarily encounter, had come to stay.

This clearly transformed the entire socialist movement. Until 1914 the moderates and the revolutionary Marxists had worked in an uneasy partnership within the ranks of nominally united parties. After the end of the war, that proved to be impossible. There had always been this cleavage between the two tendencies, from the moment that socialism had started to spread in Europe. The experiences of the war and its aftermath changed this difference into an open conflict. For the Marxists, the moderates were no longer comrades with mistaken views but were traitors whose influence on the masses was the most serious obstacle to the destined victory of the proletariat.

Conversely, the social-democrats denounced Bolshevism as tyranny and communism as a disruptive and ruinous tactic. They insisted that socialism had much more in common with liberal democracy than with the strange and seemingly ephemeral system that was being created in the East. If it came to a choice between winning power by force or remaining little more than a radical opposition in a capitalist society, they preferred the latter alternative. For, apart from the

Left socialists, who stood midway between the communists and reformists, they still did not accept the Marxist thesis that capitalism had entered a period of crisis from which there was no escape save socialism. They saw no reason why things should not continue in much the same way as before the war, with a steady increase in the socialist vote and a gradual extension of State control over private enterprise. The only danger was that communist activity might provide an excuse for restrictive or even repressive action against the whole socialist and trade union movement. They attributed the shifts in communist policy to the strong and increasing control that the Russians, through the Comintern, exerted over the smaller member parties. This, they said, made communism little more than a mere instrument of Soviet foreign policy, which could be used at Moscow's discretion to aid the friends of the Stalin régime and to attack and embarrass its enemies. Bitter experience over the years had taught social-democrats—their argument ran—that when communists embraced them it was the better to strangle them. Though many socialists rejected this sceptical approach, the dominant groups in the socialist parties found fresh evidence with each new development of communist policy to support their critical thesis.

Thus, in the years after the First World War, the history of socialism is as much a record of rivalry between communism and social-democracy as of the larger struggle of the whole movement against capitalism. It was no longer enough to agree with the broad principles of socialism. The politically-minded worker had to choose between two competing methods of achieving power.

14

THE YEARS OF CRISIS

Within two or three years of the end of the war between Germany
and the Allies the socialist movement everywhere had settled down
into a pattern that was to remain comparatively unaltered until the
development of a powerful fascist conspiracy on an international
scale created a serious threat to socialism, democracy and peace. It
was some time before the rest of the world began to establish diplomatic and trading relations with Russia, but once it was clear that
the Soviet régime could not be overthrown by foreign intervention,
and was not going to collapse of its own accord, the Bolsheviks were
left more or less alone—though everything possible was done to
isolate them—to proceed with the construction of their new social
system. They managed, however, to exercise a considerable influence
on the workers of other countries, directly through the agency of
the Comintern and its affiliated sections and, indirectly, by winning
the sympathy of many socialists who regarded Russia as the first
State run by the common people, even if these sympathisers were
not themselves prepared to accept the whole Marxist doctrine as
interpreted by Lenin.

In Germany, as we shall see below, there was a period of deadlock,
in which the Left, divided into two warring camps, was too strong to
be suppressed by the reaction and too weak to take power itself. In
Finland, Poland and the Balkans there was a dictatorship of the
Right, barely concealed behind a façade of parliamentary institutions.
Czechoslovakia, forged out of the ruins of the Hapsburg Empire,
had become a typical capitalist democracy.

In France and in Britain, which had both emerged from the war without serious internal upheavals and with their economic structure still intact, though shaken, the socialists found themselves working under much the same sort of social and political conditions as had prevailed before 1914, though their overall position was much stronger. Only in Italy, among the major States, had things taken a definite turn for the worse.

Italy, one of the weakest and most backward capitalist nations, had gained nothing of value from the war and had suffered a series of disastrous defeats. The only thing upon which the majority of Italian socialists agreed was opposition to the war. Apart from the division between the two Marxist tendencies, which existed all over Europe, the Italian labour movement had been strongly influenced by anarchism and syndicalism. When, immediately after the war, a revolutionary crisis developed, none of the various groups was itself strong enough to take the lead and none was willing to co-operate with its rivals. For a short time the workers in the North took matters into their own hands and occupied the factories. But there was no central leadership of any use and the incipient revolt petered out. The Italian Socialist Party first joined the Comintern and then quickly left it. On the Left, at a moment when everyone in Italy expected the workers to take power, there was only confusion.

It was an ideal situation for Mussolini, the former socialist journalist, and his newly-formed Fascist Party. The Italian middle-class, to say nothing of the landlords and capitalists, were terrified at the prospect of revolution, and they turned eagerly to a mass movement which seemed able to defend the interests of property. The fascists, moreover, appealed to the nationalist sentiments of a people which believed itself to have been cheated out of its legitimate reward for joining the Allies in the war. Using pseudo-socialist slogans, as the Nazis did in Germany, they were able even to get some support from the workers, who were disillusioned by the quarrels and incapacity of the parties of the Left.

With the connivance of the ruling-class Mussolini was able to seize power without any difficulty and to proceed to the suppression of all opposition to the fascist régime. In this he had the full support of the Italian capitalists, who, once they were confronted with a serious socialist challenge, found that they had little use for the trappings of democracy. They had no hesitation at all in endorsing a brutal dictatorship, for this seemed to be the only thing that could guarantee their survival.

In these circumstances there was no point in the socialists debating the respective merits of peaceful reform or revolution. The question had been settled for them. After 1925, when the fascist régime was firmly consolidated, they had to face the prospect of long years of illegal struggle.

At first fascism appeared to be a phenomenon characteristic only of Italy. But in Germany a similar movement had begun to gain ground. In its humble beginnings in Bavaria the National Socialist German Workers' Party, led by Gregor Strasser and Adolf Hitler, did not seem very different from the scores of parties which had sprung up in the Weimar Republic, consisting mainly of war veterans who hated communism, the Jews and democracy with equal venom. Germany, these said, had been betrayed by this unholy trinity, which had led the country into defeat, economic ruin and political chaos. They formed armed bands which placed themselves at the disposal of anyone, even the socialist Minister, Noske, who would offer them the opportunity to shoot or otherwise terrorise the members of the growing communist movement.

The Social-Democratic Party leaders, who had been in a position of unquestioned authority immediately after the war, found themselves drifting into coalitions with the nationalists, the Catholic Party, and conservatives. Once they had decided to adopt a policy of compromise and conciliation they found it difficult to make a stand anywhere. There was a continual threat of insurrection (doomed, in the circumstances, to result in failure and further divisions among the German workers) from the communists, whose influence among the workers increased as the socialists tried to damp down trade union activity for fear it might hamper the revival of the German economy, as they called out the police and the *Reichswehr* to break up strikes and demonstrations, and as they seemed unable to take any decisive steps to change Germany into a socialist State.

All the time the reactionaries were regaining their strength and the monopolies were extending their grip on the national economy with the assistance of the State. Most of the social-democrats, it is true, were perfectly happy at the course of events and lived in a perpetual illusion that Germany was moving steadily towards democratic socialism. But by 1931 a minority had come to realise that their party was in an intolerable position. Paralysed by the fear of Bolshevism, it had watched the Nazis, who had become the most powerful of all the movements on the extreme Right, build up an enormous machine by capitalising the hardships of the unemployed and the frustrations of the lower middle-class. They were still unable to seize power, but they managed to make a farce of German democracy.

The only thing that could have checked their progress was a united front of the two workers' parties. Though the Communist Party made repeated proposals to this effect, the social-democrats, fearing that this was merely a manœuvre to enable the communists —whose errors were certainly inexcusable in the dangerous situation —to secure control of the whole working-class movement, would have nothing to do with the idea. The mutual recriminations which came after the Nazis had taken power testify to the mistakes made by both wings of the labour movement. As the communists were to admit at the 1935 congress of the Comintern, they sought a united front *only from below*, and had taken too sharp a line against the socialist leaders—a mistake that stemmed from the overall Comintern strategy for Europe and from an underestimation of the loyalty of the socialist rank-and-file to its leaders and the strength of the joint fascist-nationalist revival. Socialists, however, saw that they reaped the fruits of their failure to break German reaction when they had the chance at the end of the war; they had left the capitalists and landlords in undisputed possession of their property and their reward was to see the industrialists openly subsidizing the Nazis, the nationalists calling for the repudiation of the Treaty of Versailles and the rearmament of Germany, and all the reactionary parties insisting that they should acquiesce in the suppression of the communists and the militant trade union movement.

The Weimar Republic, on which the social-democrats had pinned all their hopes, was already tottering when the world economic crisis of 1931 dealt it a death-blow. As the unemployment figures soared, so the Nazis and the Communist Party gained ground, each racing to inherit the collapsing régime. Riots and street fighting became a common occurrence. The Social-Democratic Party and the other Centre groups were slowly being ground to pieces between the two extremes. They had completely lost the initiative. It was by then too late to undo the errors of the previous ten years. If another revolutionary crisis developed, they had no hope of riding the storm as they had in 1918. They could counsel moderation, as they had done so often in the past, but their advice was unlikely to carry much weight. Parliamentary democracy had failed in Germany and the leaders of the Social-Democratic Party were tarred with its discredit. They had to meet the communist charge that they had once more betrayed the working-class, as they had during the war, by allying themselves with reactionary parties and defending, instead of eliminating, capitalism. In reply, the socialists insisted that the communists were most to blame for the disintegration of the republic, for they had consistently attacked the democratic institutions created at Weimar as a sham, kept the country in a continuous state of unrest and, by raising the spectre of the proletarian revolution, provoked the counter-revolution which now threatened. Wherever the responsibility actually rested, these recriminations were no defence against the skilful agitation of the Nazis, who exploited the division of the workers' movement to their own advantage.

The social-democrats and the liberals hesitated to take the emergency power needed to suppress the Nazis, lest they were accused of destroying the last remnants of the democracy they were struggling to keep alive. The communists alone, and themselves subject to police persecution, were not strong enough to forestall the Nazis. Some communist functionaries, moreover, were under the fatal delusion that if the Nazis came to power the workers who remained under social-democratic influence would at least realise the futility of reformism and would rally to the Communist Party, which would then lead a successful insurrection.

At the beginning of 1933 the Nazis were the strongest single party in the Reichstag, and Adolf Hitler was Chancellor. Seizing the excuse of anp imending communist revolt—of which only they were able to see any evidence—the Nazis took complete power. First, they suppressed the Communist Party; the Social-Democratic Party and the free trade unions shortly suffered the same fate, though some social-democrats at first tried to save themselves by giving conditional support to Hitler's foreign policy. In a short time the once impressive German working-class movement was in ruins and its leaders were either on the run or in the new concentration camps set up by the Nazis. Between them the communists and socialists had polled more than twelve million votes at the last elections, yet when the crisis came in 1933 they were not able even to call a general strike, let alone organise armed resistance to the Nazis. Too many of the workers had been deceived by fascist propaganda into believing that the Nazis really intended to carry through the anti-capitalist revolution which the Social-Democratic Party had not attempted and the Communist Party had been unable to accomplish.

Shortly after Germany went fascist a parallel attack was launched on the Austrian socialists by Dollfuss. In spite of the heroic fight put up by the workers of Vienna, they, too, had left resistance too late. In crushing the Austrian Left, the clerical reactionaries opened the way for the annexation of their country by Germany four years later, in 1938.

Thus, throughout Central and Eastern Europe, where the democratic tradition had never been very strong, the reactionary social forces were steadily regaining the positions from which they had been driven immediately after 1918. Even before the great economic crisis of the 'thirties they had made a striking recovery, but after the onset of the depression they went over to the offensive, and one after another the bastions of democracy began to fall.

There were a few countries, however, where events had not taken such an unhappy course. In Scandinavia, for instance, the socialist parties polled more votes with every election. They neither threatened violence themselves nor encountered it from their opponents. They had long ago rejected the Marxist doctrine of bitter class-war, believing that constitutional reform was both desirable and practicable in nations where the workers enjoyed a comparatively high standard of living, where there was no large class of wealthy and usurious capitalists, and where a high proportion of the population lived on the land. They also found that, on specific issues, they were on common ground with the other big parties. There was no furious opposition to the development of trade unions or of the co-operative movement: they were not alone in demanding free and efficient educational, medical and other social services; they had no desire to expropriate either landlords or capitalists in order merely to satisfy a dogmatic principle. In short, they worked as radical reformers.

They were the kind of socialist parties of which the Fabians and Bernstein had dreamed. Peaceful, respectable and painstaking in their attention to administrative detail, they justly took credit for their share in making the Scandinavian countries a model of healthy and progressive democracy in which both State control and private enterprise could find a place. The socialists had not been involved in the catastrophe of 1914–18, and they were thus able to combine pacifism with patriotism. They was no reason to revile employers who ran their industries efficiently and treated their workers well. They did not bother much with agricultural questions, for there was no large rural proletariat clamouring for a division of the land, and the farmers themselves showed a preference for co-operative methods.

It was true that a completely socialist society was still a long way off, but the socialists saw no need to hurry. Their countries were prosperous economically and politically stable. Why should they risk all that had already been achieved by the hard work of two generations? Premature socialisation would only antagonise many people who were willing to support a comprehensive programme of reform, but who did not wish to undermine a capitalist system which was both flexible and successful.

Due to the special conditions of the Scandinavian States, this policy of compromise and gradualism did not lead the socialist movement into serious difficulties. If no substantial advance was made towards the traditional goal of socialism, the Scandinavian socialist parties were at least able to deal effectively with social problems such as housing and unemployment.

Much the same sort of thing happened in Switzerland. Though the Belgian and Dutch social-democrats would have liked to follow a similar policy, it was not quite so easy for them. Both countries had large colonial empires and their economies were peculiarly responsive to fluctuations in world trade; in both there were considerable religious minorities, and the labour movement, as well as other parties, tended to divide along religious as much as social lines. In Belgium, especially, there was a continual undercurrent of industrial unrest, and it was not possible to dismiss the Marxist analysis of capitalism as totally irrelevant to the conditions of the Belgian working-class.

The Low Countries, perched on the fringes of France and Germany, also had to take account of what was happening to their bigger neighbours. As soon as the threat of a new war developed, the defence of their neutrality took priority over differences about domestic policy. Even if the social-democrats had managed to win a decisive electoral majority in either Holland or Belgium, it is doubtful whether they would have been able to do more than nationalise one or two industries and carry through a few reforms unless at least one important State in Europe had also gone over to a radical form of socialism. For they lived always in the shadow of events beyond their control.

Russia, with its immense resources, could risk isolation and hostility. A small nation, dependent upon the trade and friendship of great capitalist countries, was not entirely the master of its own destiny. The socialists had to wait and, with the exception of a minority on the extreme Left, they were not unduly dissatisfied with their progress.

In a large part of Europe the World War ended in chaos and revolutionary upheavals. Britain, however, emerged from the conflict with its economic system still intact, though weakened. In spite of the militancy displayed by a section of the workers, this industrial agitation never looked like a serious preparation for insurrection. But the war, all the same, had changed the face of British politics. The swing to the Left, so much more pronounced on the Continent, had broken the hold that the Liberal Party had hitherto possessed on progressive opinion in Britain. As the Labour Party, which had been the third and junior partner in the wartime Coalition Government, began to attract a majority of the workers and some of the middle-class, and, consequently, to take the place of the Liberals as the champion of steady constitutional reform, so the Right wing of the Liberal Party moved over to the Conservatives, who were much more capable of defending the interests of property against further encroachments.

At the same time, the long years of socialist propaganda had begun to bear fruit. The trade unions no longer objected to the party which their funds supported adopting a nominally socialist programme. Indeed, as we have seen, some of the unions had already come out openly for the overthrow of capitalism during the syndicalist agitation which had preceded the war. In 1918, when the Labour Party at last drafted a formal programme, *Labour and the New Social Order*, it was thereby committed to socialism, though the word appeared nowhere in the draft. Simultaneously, it was decided to admit individual members to the party and to form local branches in every possible constituency. Up to this point the party had consisted of members affiliated through a trade union or through one of the small socialist organisations. This reorganisation completed, it was ready to make a bid for a majority in Parliament.

The Labour Party now stood squarely upon its own feet. But the socialism which it had made its official policy was still the brand supplied by the Fabian Society. Though the influence of the Marxists had increased as a result of the war and of the Russian revolution, they had formed themselves into a distinct Communist Party which was violently criticising—and was, in turn, criticised by—the moderate socialists. It was impossible for two groups so bitterly opposed to live together, and before long the communists were driven right out of the Labour Party and there was no nucleus around which effective opposition to the reformist policy of MacDonald and his associates could crystallise. The latter had things all their own way in the party when they insisted that, whatever the situation might be in Europe, in Britain there was no reason to question the possibility of using the ordinary constitutional machinery for the gradual introduction of socialism. Indeed, Sidney Webb, the most prominent theoretician of the Fabians, coined the phrase 'the inevitability of gradualness' to sum up the Labour Party's philosophy.

The Labour Party, in 1923, won just under two hundred seats and became the official Opposition. When, in the following January, the Tory Government was turned out by a combined vote of the Liberals and Labour, Ramsay MacDonald agreed to form a minority Labour administration with the support—but not the participation —of the Liberals. Though this Government had some things to its credit, notably John Wheatley's Housing Act and its treatment of the unemployed, it could not live. For nine months the MacDonald Cabinet was wholly dependent upon the goodwill of the Liberals, and when this was withdrawn it collapsed. At the election which followed the Conservatives capitalised on the 'Red Scare' produced by the Zinoviev Letter and won more than four hundred seats. Labour representation fell to a hundred and fifty—though the total Labour vote rose by more than a million—while the Liberals were almost wiped out.

It was soon clear that this electoral defeat was but the prelude to a general attack upon the whole working-class movement. British capitalism was in an extremely difficult position. It had lost its old supremacy in the world market as a direct result of the war. It was saddled with debt and obsolete plant. It had failed to improve its technique to meet the challenge of new competitors. If it was to regain a large part of its losses it had somehow to reduce its costs. The most simple and obvious way to do this was to cripple the trade unions and thus check their wage demands. The industrial picture, indeed, was very dismal. The miners, who had hoped for the national-isation of the collieries after 1919, when the Sankey Commission recommended it by the chairman's casting vote, were engaged in a long guerilla struggle with their masters. In other industries there was a growing strike wave. And in every large town there were long queues of unemployed outside the labour exchanges.

By 1926 a crisis had been reached. The trade union movement decided that it would call a general strike in support of the miners. The trade union leaders, however, had very little idea of where this strike might lead, for they regarded the strike as a purely economic weapon. It was intended to be a demonstration of proletarian solidarity, and when it actually started in May it fulfilled this limited purpose effectively. But it was doomed to futility, once the British ruling class decided to resist it to the bitter end, using force to suppress it if necessary, unless its leaders were prepared to carry things to the point of revolution. As soon as this was brought home to them they capitulated immediately, leaving the miners to their fate.

Peace had been secured, though at a high price. For the way was now open for the restrictive legislation, embodied in the Trades Disputes Act of 1927, which the employers desired. This Act, moreover, served a double aim. By altering the basis on which unions collected their political funds it struck a severe blow at the finances of the Labour Party—a handicap which remained until the Act was repealed after Labour's victory in 1945.

It is surprising that this experience did not produce any fundamental change in the attitude of the British socialists towards the State. On the one occasion when they had presented a major challenge to the rights and security of capitalist property, every possible instrument of coercion had been mobilised against them. Yet in the years after 1926 MacDonald and his colleagues showed no sign that they had learnt anything from the crisis. On the contrary, they kept their eyes fixed on the goal of office and never questioned the assumptions on which all their activities were based.

It would have been better for the Labour Party if it had taken stock of its position in the late 'twenties. It might then have avoided a second fiasco. But neither the defeat of 1924, nor the General Strike, nor the fall in union membership from over eight to under four millions, between 1920 and 1929, produced any effective challenge to the policy pursued by MacDonald and his friends. MacDonald himself had been caught up in the confusion of his phrase-mongering and had lost whatever sense of reality he had ever possessed. It is not surprising he led his party steadily towards disaster instead of socialism. For socialism, to him, had nothing to do with the struggle of the working-class against capitalism but was 'the rise of social unity and growth towards organic wholeness', which could only succeed if the workers condemned the class-struggle.

When, early in 1929, Labour emerged from the elections as the largest party, though it was still in a minority in Parliament, Mac-Donald had no hesitation in repeating the disastrous experiment of 1924, accepting office without power by the grace of the Liberals. Apart from its failure to deal with unemployment effectively, which aroused serious criticism within the Labour Party, the government carried through some respectable legislation, and it had a good record on foreign affairs, but its standing was never sure. Once the great economic depression started, it was helpless. It was not strong enough to undertake any substantial changes in the structure of British society, even if it had desired, and such changes could not, in any case, have been made in time to ward off the worst effects of the crisis. It was consequently driven into an attempt to hold together the stricken capitalist system to whose eventual abolition it was committed. In this task, naturally, it encountered the hostility and obstruction of the employers, who believed that their interests would be better served by their own representatives in the Conservative Party. MacDonald, who was in a panic, was persuaded without much difficulty to desert his party and without its prior knowledge he formed a new National government. It is a measure of the suspicion with which he was by this time regarded by most of his party that he was able to carry no more than a handful of its members with him.

But loyalty to socialist principles did not save the Labour Party from an overwhelming rout at the elections which followed. By 1931 it had no more Members of Parliament than it had had in 1918. The Conservatives were firmly in the saddle again, and once the immediate crisis had been weathered they were able to devote themselves to bolstering up British industry and agriculture by extensive subsidies, and by the encouragement of monopolies. In the subsequent economy drive it was not only wages that were cut. Expenditure on all social services was drastically reduced. But though a new wave of militancy swept through the Labour movement—reinforced by the agitation of millions of unemployed—there was little the working-class could do. Its party was in the wilderness, and it was to remain there all through the critical years when capitalism all over the world was passing through its most critical phase and when the development of the fascist menace was raising new and complex problems for socialists everywhere.

THE TOTALITARIAN THIRTIES

The period between the Wall Street crash in 1929 and the outbreak of World War II was a decade in which democracy was on the defensive. Economically, it was a period of depression, of low agricultural prices and high unemployment: there was little improvement until the middle of the decade, when rearmament began to increase demand for raw materials and to stimulate the economies of the major industrial powers. In many ways this collapse seemed to bear out the classic socialist case against capitalism—that it could not cure the trade cycle, or deal with poverty and inequality, or use the idle factories and unsold food crops. Yet the crisis only made recruits for socialist movements (and turned many intellectuals to Marxism); it did not lead anywhere to the expected socialist revolution. The only democratic country that made a spectacular attempt to deal with its social problems, in fact, was the USA, through the New Deal launched by President Franklin D. Roosevelt—and this was the one large capitalist country where the socialist movement was weak, and where even the trade union movement had to wait for the New Deal legislation to achieve mass membership.

Politically, the changes that occurred were far from those that socialists had expected from a full-scale capitalist depression. It was not the Left-wing parties that made real headway, but the Right-wing authoritarian movements such as the Nazis in Germany, the fascists in Italy, Austria and Spain, and the aggressive militarist faction in Japan. The fascist trend, moreover, was not confined to the domestic

politics of these countries. Hitler's Germany was openly expansion-
ist. First the Rhineland, then the Saar, then Austria and Czechoslovakia, fell to Hitler without a shot being fired; Mussolini conquered
Ethiopia; Japan absorbed Manchuria and began the long war
against a weak China. Fascist movements, enjoying support from
Germany and Italy, grew up even in the democratic countries.

In such circumstances, two things happened to socialists. The first
was that they began to think less and less of the ways in which they
might achieve socialism, and more of the need to defend the frontiers
of democracy. The second was that even non-communists began to
look more sympathetically at what was happening in the Soviet
Union—or at what they believed was happening. As we shall see
below, the two things were not synonymous. But the Soviet Union
had become an emotionally-charged symbol for the Left as a whole,
not merely for communists. No matter what frustrations or defeats
there might be, there was always one place to which a Left-winger
could look with hope and enthusiasm. In Russia, socialism seemed
to work; in Soviet diplomacy, there was a steady advocate of collective security against aggression; in the Red Army, there was the
one military force which could withstand the legions of Hitler and
Mussolini. Such feelings, furthermore, were reinforced by other
factors: the capitalist crisis had given greater plausibility to the
Marxist diagnosis, and—after years of sectarian strife—local communist parties were making new overtures for 'anti-fascist' unity
with other sections of the organised labour movement.

Later events were to show how much wishful thinking lay behind
the apparent realism of such views. Increasingly, the dark side of the
Soviet system—terror and concentration camps—became evident;
in 1956, in his celebrated 'secret speech' to the 20th party congress,
Nikita Krushchev confirmed criticisms of Stalin's régime that, in
the mood of the 'thirties, had been dismissed as mere anti-Soviet
calumnies. In 1939, when Stalin signed a pact with Hitler, collective
security collapsed overnight, and it was the Polish, French, Belgian,
Norwegian, Dutch and British armies that fought the first campaigns
of World War II. In retrospect, Stalin's totalitarian tyranny seems
to make a mockery of the propaganda of the 'thirties. But, to understand what happened before and during World War II, it is essential

to realise how much of that propaganda was taken at face value. Some socialists, it is true, remained anti-communist, pointing out the evils of Stalinist society and the duplicity of communist tactics. But they were a minority: the majority preferred a simplified picture of the world, in which the Soviet Union stood as the champion of peace, freedom and progress against the fascist menace—while the democratic (or 'imperialist') powers hovered uneasily between appeasement of the fascist aggressors and preparation to fight them.

Conceptions of this kind dominated the Left in the 'thirties, and were most dramatically expressed in the policy of the Popular Front. This policy was one of the more ingenious and successful ideas of the Communist International—a body not greatly distinguished by original thought or practical achievement. For the first time since the Russian Revolution it enabled the communists to break out of their sectarian isolation and exercise considerable influence over wide sections of the socialist and trade union movement. Like most communist policies, its primary purpose was to serve the interests of the Soviet Union; but because it was moderate in character, and focussed effectively on the pressing need to mobilise resistance to fascism, it provided a formula which—with a significant and damaging interlude between 1939 and 1941—was to dominate Left-wing politics until the outbreak of the Cold War in 1947.

What happened within the Soviet system to produce this change? All through the 'twenties there had been a fierce tactical struggle between Stalin, on the one hand, and Trotsky on the other. Stalin had taken power when it became clear that the upheavals that followed World War I were not leading to any revolutionary victory outside Russia; the communist régime could not count on support from any more industrialised country, and it therefore had to build up its own industry. The construction of an industrial base, and the collectivisation of agriculture, thus became the main objectives of Stalin's policy. Trotsky, however, had lost the fight for power: believing that a backward country such as Russia could not build a socialist society without outside help, he had opposed Stalin's doctrine of 'socialism in one country' and insisted that this would lead to a bureaucratic dictatorship. It is important to note that as early as 1905, Trotsky had had reservations about Lenin's concept of 'democratic centralism'—the principle on which the Bolshevik Party was organised. It would, he said, lead first to the dictatorship of the proletariat over the country as a whole; next to the dictatorship of the party over the proletariat; then to the dictatorship of the central committee over the party; and finally to the dictatorship of one man over the central committee.

Trotsky lived to see this sad prophecy come true, and he was luckier than most of Stalin's opponents. By 1934 Stalin had defeated Trotsky and his followers (who had become convinced that the Soviet system was not socialist at all but a form of State capitalism), and he then went on to liquidate all his critics—and tens of thousands of Soviet citizens who were merely the luckless objects of paranoid suspicion. One measure of the purges which went on throughout the 'thirties with increasing ferocity was the fate of the delegates to the 17th party congress in 1934. More than 70 per cent of the central committee members then elected were shot within two or three years; of the 1,966 delegates, at least 1,108 were condemned for 'counter-revolutionary' activity. Another crucial illustration reveals how Stalin destroyed the officer corps of the Soviet army—one reason why, perhaps, he had to make a panic and temporary truce with Hitler immediately afterwards, and also one explanation of the mishandling of the Soviet troops in the first months after Hitler's attack. After Stalin's death, Krushchev reported, a special military tribunal 'rehabilitated 7,679 persons, many of whom were rehabilitated posthumously'.

Stalin, to put matters briefly, had become obsessed by problems of security—internal and external. His régime had real material achievements to its credit, though these had been won at great human loss. But while the achievements were extolled throughout the world, the cost was minimised; socialists and communists alike needed to believe that all was well in the Soviet Union, and that the purges were a justified form of protection against fascist disruption and espionage. Some people, it is true, did ask why old and tried members of the Bolshevik Party such as Zinoviev, Kamenev and Bukharin—all former colleagues of Lenin—should suddenly become fascist agents. But even such critics were inhibited by the fact that the Soviet Union, diplomatically, and the Communist International politically, were seemingly taking the initiative in opposing fascism. For Stalin, fearing that Russia might be attacked by the Germans, the Japanese, or both, was trying to find allies—and this need dictated a change of policy. At the very moment when he was beginning a draconian terror within the Soviet Union, he was assuming the mask of moderation towards the outside world. He could not hope to win the co-operation of Britain, France and the USA—in each country, an influential minority would have been well pleased to see the fascists attack an isolated USSR—if he maintained a sectarian foreign policy, and if communists in such countries were attacking the very politicians whom he was trying to woo.

In foreign affairs the new policy had already been adopted by 1934, when the USSR became willing to enter into alliances and agreements with capitalist states (in that year, Russia joined the League of Nations), to foster the idea of collective security, and to encourage the national sections of the Comintern to give conditional support to governments which would co-operate with Moscow. In domestic policy it meant that communists would refrain from putting forward demands which would isolate them from all except a radical fringe; their task was to draft a minimum programme of social reform as the basis upon which anti-fascist unity could be built.

The seal was set on this change by the Seventh World Congress of the Communist International, held in Moscow in 1935. At this meeting, Georgi Dimitrov, the Bulgarian who had become general secretary of the Comintern after his successful defiance of the Nazis on the charge of burning down the Reichstag in 1933, laid down the guiding lines of the new policy. The struggle against fascism was the first priority, he said; wherever possible communists and social-democrats should form alliances, since only a united working-class movement could prevent a repetition of the German catastrophe in one place after another. It would be folly, Dimitrov argued, to raise the question of the transition to socialism; if the fascists should triumph, there would be neither bourgeois democracy nor socialism. The Popular Front, therefore, must be based on the working-class movement, but it should endeavour to influence all democrats, irrespective of party.

Although, in the countries under fascist rule, social-democrats had

F

suffered equally with communists, the parties of the Second International were slow to find an effective response. The International itself was an amorphous body, lacking the centralised control of the Comintern; and the social-democrats were understandably dubious about the new communist line, regarding it as simply another manœuvre designed to enable the communists to seize control of the working-class movement. Yet, while resisting formal association with the communists, the social-democrats found it hard to devise a policy that differed significantly from that now proposed in Moscow. It was plain sense to minimise sectarian socialist demands, and to seek the widest possible coalition of forces against the fascists. Thus the leaders of social-democratic groups, such as the British Labour Party, were hard put to it to find good reasons why their supporters should not respond to the communist proposals for united action. They might, from long experience, doubt the integrity of the communists; but it was difficult to prove that the tactics they advocated were undesirable.

They appeared so desirable, in fact, that the Popular Front movement slowly gained ground. France, for example, was threatened by a resurgent Germany, by an active and dangerous fascist conspiracy from within, and by a serious economic crisis. In the seventeen years after 1918, the Left had never been strong enough to secure a majority in the Chamber of Deputies; but in 1936 an electoral alliance between the Socialist Party, the Radicals and the communists swept a Socialist-Radical coalition into office. At the same time, the two national trade union centres—one of which was non-political and the other led by communists—fused into a united CGT. In 1934, France had seemed to be on the verge of a fascist coup; during 1936, the propertied French feared that the revolution was at hand. All over the country, in a series of great strikes, workers occupied factories and offices, refusing to vacate them until their demands were met.

This movement to the Left secured concessions, especially in social legislation, but it also evoked a quick reaction. Financial interests apparently engineered a currency crisis, and refused to take any steps to deal with it until the Popular Front government agreed to moderate its social programme and hand over the leadership of the government to the Radicals. From that point onwards the Left became the prisoner of its Radical allies. It was well aware that if it pressed its demands too hard, the alliance would be broken, and a reactionary régime would come to power. Had it not been for the grave external threat of fascism, the socialists and communists might have taken the risk of an open confrontation with the Right. But, with the example of Spain before them, this was a risk that seemed too great.

For, in Spain, a complex revolutionary war was in progress. After the fall of the Spanish monarchy in 1931, the Socialist Party had become the single strongest group in Spain: and in the elections of March 1936, a Spanish Popular Front had won a sweeping victory. Though the communists were at this time a small minority, and though the socialists did not even participate in the new government, the prospect of agrarian and social reform was enough to start a civil war. In July, monarchist army officers, with German and Italian backing, began an insurrection. It is interesting to note that, in the last years of his life, Marx had at least considered that such a pattern might be more likely than a proletarian revolution—that progressive forces might win an election, and then be faced with an armed counter-revolutionary threat.

Certainly, the Republican régime in Spain was legally and popularly elected; and all over the world it found support among democrats and progressives—many of whom sent foodstuffs and medical supplies to its aid, and some of whom went to Spain to fight as volunteers in the International Brigade. Though the communists became increasingly influential (helped by limited Russian military aid), and succeeded in destroying the anarchist and syndicalist parties on the grounds that their 'revolutionary leftism' was objectively aiding the fascists, the cause of Spain became the cause of all anti-fascists. This was partly because Spain was the first occasion on which democrats had chosen to stand and fight against fascists, rather than appease them. But there were more complex reasons why the Spanish war was symbolic. It summed up in one sad history all the problems which confronted the Left in this period. Did it mean, for instance, that even a moderate republican government would be overthrown by armed reaction, with support from the fascist states? If so, what were the prospects of a peaceful transition to socialism? Did the failure of the British, French and American governments to aid the Spanish Republic mean that they would continue to let the fascists dismember Europe? If so, what were the prospects of collective security, or a working alliance against Hitler and Mussolini? Could pacifists support even so necessary a war? And if they could not, what useful contribution could they make to a Labour Party such as that in Britain which, with strong pacifist traditions, was nevertheless faced by the need to resist the dictators? Should the struggle against fascism be broadly based, with very little attempt to change the social order—as Popular Front policies would have it—or should it be transformed into a revolutionary struggle, as the Spanish anarchists, syndicalists and Trotskyists had vainly argued? How far, once the fighting began, would communists tend to take control? How far, indeed, could they be trusted by their allies? How much practical aid was Stalin prepared to give, and how far would he subordinate the interests of any anti-fascist group to the needs of Soviet diplomacy?

All these and similar questions were raised by the Spanish campaign, and the last of them was a vital one. The point had already been raised in China, where Stalin's theoretical incapacity and his diplomatic urgencies had long ago led him to give advice to the Chinese communists which, if they had followed it, would probably have led to the destruction of their movement. Mao Tse-tung made his revolution by ignoring Stalin. Later, both the Yugoslavs under Marshal Tito (during World War II), and the July 26 movement led by Castro in Cuba, made their revolutions by rejecting the official communist line. On the contrary, the well-disciplined French and Italian communist parties—which had virtual control of the resistance movements in their countries—made no attempt to seize power when liberation came. It is true that Allied armies occupied both countries, but the presence of British troops in Athens had not prevented Greek leftists from attempting to take over in the winter of 1944–5. Wherever Stalin's writ ran, communists served his interests first, their own seldom.

As late as 1939, however, communists were still making headway as the most energetic opponents of fascism, just as the Soviet Union was gaining prestige for the same reason; but since they played down radical demands in the interests of unity, their success was essentially tactical. True, Marxism was becoming influential as a theory, and the apparent successes of the Soviet Union offered evidence for the viability of socialism. Yet, even in the late 'thirties, one of the reasons advanced by the British Labour leaders for refusing to co-operate in a Popular Front movement was that the communists wanted to associate with such bourgeois groups as the Liberals.

The Labour Party itself had made little progress. Its leaders insisted that they could only win a majority in Britain if they were able to present themselves to the country as a safe and responsible alternative government which, on winning office, would not engage in a wholesale assault on capitalism but would advance gradually towards socialism by a series of reforms, none of which would frighten moderate opinion, and each of which would appear desirable in its own right as a means of alleviating poverty, inequality of opportunity, and economic inefficiency. In foreign affairs, though they strongly supported the idea of collective security organised through the League of Nations, they had to take account of a strong pacifist element in the party: the pacifist influence, coupled with a deep suspicion that rearmament was designed to bolster British imperialism rather than oppose fascism, made things difficult for those in the party who urged a stronger stand in international affairs.

This cautious policy had not yielded any sensational results at the 1935 General Election, when Labour did little more than re-establish itself in its old strongholds in the mining and heavy industrial areas. But the deteriorating international situation began to provide the party leadership with strong arguments against the pacifist wing; at the same time, the leaders managed to steer clear of any association with the communists, believing that this would be damaging to their efforts to win the middle-class vote. They were even hesitant to come out strongly in support of the Spanish Republicans.

In 1937, a new Labour programme was drafted, setting out the measures that a Labour government would take after winning an election: it was notable for its moderation, and for its rejection of the much more radical policies which had been adopted in the aftermath of MacDonald's defection. The substance of this programme

was discussed by the party's new leader, Clement Attlee, in a book
called *The Labour Party in Perspective*: eight years later, when
Labour had at last won a dramatic election victory, Attlee formed a
government whose legislative programme so closely resembled that
set out in his book that some of the measures were actually enacted
in the order he then proposed.

The 'thirties were generally a period of retreat for the socialist
movement. It produced no significant new ideas, beyond the communist tactic of the Popular Front; it failed to cope successfully
with the problems set by the capitalist crisis and the advance of
fascism; and even the much-heralded success of the Soviet Union
must be regarded not so much as a success for socialism—as tradition-
ally conceived—as for the building of an industrial society by totalitarian methods.

These failures were made more pointed in the 'thirties, moreover,
by events in the United States, the one country where there was
neither an important socialist nor a powerful trade union movement.
After World War I, the socialist vote had dwindled, and the trade
unions had remained a small proportion of the total work force.
Yet, after the election of Franklin D. Roosevelt as President in
1932, the United States not only produced the dramatic social and
economic measures known as the New Deal; it also saw the rise of
a new and powerful trade union movement, known as the Congress
of Industrial Organisations. It is an interesting question why
America should have proved the exception to the general decline of
democracy and radicalism in this period.

The question, indeed, can be put in another form. Why was it that
the USA, with a strong democratic tradition, and with the most
advanced forms of industrial capitalism, should have failed to produce a powerful labour or socialist party? In terms of classical
Marxist ideas, it should have done so—yet American progressivism
has always taken a different course.

During the nineteenth century, when waves of European immigrants poured into the USA, many socialists went too: in the last
stages of the First International, in fact, its headquarters were transferred to New York. But these immigrants, in ideas and in organisation, looked backwards to Europe; many of them could not even

speak English, and as late as 1914 a majority of the active members in the American Socialist Party were foreign-born. They never succeeded in reaching out to American workers in a decisive way; for one thing, in a country where there had been a tradition of opportunity, based upon free land, these workers did not form a proletariat in the European sense; for another, despite recurrent crises, American capitalism had been able to offer a rising standard of life to many millions. American politics, moreover, fitted a different pattern. A huge country, where government was divided between federal and state legislatures, it was ruled by two large parties which were quite unlike European parties in structure or ideological outlook. The differences between them were often less important than the differences within them; the parties were much more like coalitions welded together by informal alliances, permitting them to appeal to all kinds of interests and enabling the changing currents of public opinion to flow through them. For constitutional and political reasons too complex to discuss here, American radicalism had always found it easier to seek expression through these political machines than to set up a new one in opposition to them. Repeated attempts to found a separate radical party (the latest was in 1948, when former vice-president Henry Wallace ran for president on a Progressive ticket) had always foundered, and the radicals either wandered off into a sectarian wilderness or returned to the conventional parties.

From 1932, most liberals and radicals found a suitable home in the Democratic Party, which now stood for a series of social reforms, including the advancement of trade unionism. Roosevelt had built an electoral alliance which appealed to poor farmers, industrial workers, the Negroes, and substantial numbers of shopkeepers and white collar workers who were suffering from the depression. The legislation he sponsored gave substantial government aid to rural areas, guaranteed trade union rights, established such large-scale government enterprises as the Tennessee Valley Authority, provided basic social services, and set up public works projects to relieve unemployment. This was not a socialist programme; but it achieved more than most moderate socialist parties had ever been able to achieve.

Roosevelt was also strongly opposed to fascism. Strong isolationist pressures made it difficult for him to become directly involved in diplomatic resistance either to the European fascists or to Japanese aggression in the Far East. The United States was able to enter World War II only after Japan had attacked Pearl Harbor in 1941. But there was never any doubt that the Roosevelt administration was prepared to defend democratic institutions; and from 1936 onwards rearmament had begun in the United States—a policy of preparedness that was to pay decisive dividends in the coming war.

As late as 1939, however, America still seemed remote from the concerns of Europe—and few European socialists asked how relevant the American experience was to the problems facing them. One of them, John Strachey—a man who probably did more to popularise Marxism in the English language than any other person —did change his mind. At the very end of the decade, after writing such famous expositions of Marxism as *The Theory and Practice of Socialism*, he changed his mind, and in a book called *Programme for Progress* he urged socialists to profit from the American lesson. But by then the war had already begun.

Strachey, like many other sympathisers with communism and the Soviet Union, had been outraged by the non-aggression pact that Stalin had signed with Hitler in 1939. After several years of denouncing fascism, and insisting that the Soviet Union would be in the vanguard of any military campaign against the aggressors, communists had suddenly to make a complete volte-face: all the anti-fascist slogans were dropped, and for two years the parties of the Communist International followed defeatist policies which antagonised their erstwhile allies and hampered the war effort against Hitler and Mussolini. It may be easy, today, to see why this change occurred. Stalin's Russia was poorly prepared for war; even two years later, the Nazi armies came within a few miles of taking Moscow, and only the early onset of winter saved the Red Army from overwhelming defeat. It seems, furthermore, that Stalin feared that the British and the French were seeking to manœuvre him into a position where Russia might have to fight alone against Germany—and possibly Japan. One can only guess at what might have happened had he not made this panicky attempt to buy vital time. There is no need to guess at the effect it had on the communist movement, which was forced to reveal that it put the interest of Stalin's Russia above all other considerations.

Years later, Stalin was grudgingly forced to concede that the anti-Hitler war had been an anti-fascist war from the beginning, though paradoxically it had been waged in the first instance by the bourgeois powers who had seemed so hesitant to resist the aggressors in the 'thirties. But until 1941, communists had no part in it. It was only after Hitler's attack on the Soviet Union in July of that year that communists in all the occupied countries revived the tactics of the Popular Front under a new name—the National Front—and sought to take a leading role in the resistance movements that grew up. Their courage and organisational skill enabled them to recover much of the ground lost by the Nazi–Soviet pact; and they were helped by the heroic and immensely costly sacrifices that the Russian people made to destroy the bulk of the Nazi armies. During these years, when the old state structures and political parties were smashed by fascist occupation, when patriotism and radicalism could be combined in the struggle for national liberation, all Europe moved leftwards.

No one could predict what shape this new Europe would take. Much was to depend, in the event, on military operations (and political agreements such as those made between the great powers at Teheran and Yalta) which decided what parts of Europe would be liberated by British and American armies, and what by Soviet troops —or, in the case of Yugoslavia, by a powerful guerilla movement led by the old Comintern organiser, Josip Broz, now called Marshal Tito. Yet it was certain that the defeat of fascism would usher in a new and quite different phase in the evolution of socialism: there were few pessimists who foresaw that the euphoria and unity of the war years would rapidly give way to a new struggle, more bitter than any earlier division between social-democrats and communists— the Cold War.

16

THE SOCIALIST PARADOX

Engels once wrote that 'anyone who says that a socialist revolution can be carried out in a country which has no proletariat or bourgeoisie proves by this statement that he has still to learn the ABC of socialism'. Yet, as we noted in the opening chapter of this book, the paradox of socialism is that its successes have been in precisely those societies where capitalism was weak, where the proletariat scarcely existed, and where the revolution has been made by an alliance of intellectuals with land-hungry peasants. Socialist measures have not come as a response to industrialism, but rather as a means of achieving it by totalitarian methods.

This was true of the Soviet Union, which as late as 1939 was the only country claiming to be socialist; it is also true of the countries that were added to the 'socialist camp' after World War II—the régimes of East Europe, China, North Korea and North Vietnam, and Cuba. Much the same point can be made about several of the new 'non-aligned' nations, such as Indonesia, Algeria and Ghana. Though many of the older industrialised states have come to accept far-reaching policies of welfare and social reform, of a type long advocated by the traditional working-class movements, and though by 1965 Britain was ruled by its fourth Labour government, not one of these states has experienced a socialist revolution of the kind envisaged by Marx and the other founders of modern socialism.

Such a paradox is so striking that it puts almost all the theories described in this book in a different perspective. While the new revolutionary movements claim descent from Marx (and we should note how strenuously Communist China claims to be the guardian of Marxist orthodoxy), they are in fact a quite new phenomenon. They may retain Marx's theory of history in a modified form; they may insist on extensive public ownership of land and industry; they may introduce centralised planning of the economy, and retain the rhetoric of fraternity and internationalism. But the differences between them and the workers' movement in industrial countries are so great that it is worth asking whether there is much point in continuing to treat them under the same general heading of 'socialism'. Can we easily stretch the meaning of the word to describe societies as dissimilar as contemporary Britain and modern China, or organisations so unlike as the Swedish Social Democratic Party and the Convention People's Party of Ghana? How much of Marx's theory of society remains when we note that many of its crucial assertions about industrial capitalism have proved false, and that it has won decisive support only in societies unlike those it purported to describe?

Such questions are not altogether new; even in the nineteenth century, when various kinds of socialist theory and organisation were competing for leadership of the working-class movement, and when that movement was largely confined to Europe, some perspicacious critics—such as Bernstein—had begun to raise them. They became more relevant after 1917, when the common ancestry of Leninist communism and social-democracy proved less significant than their practical divergences. But since 1945 they cannot be evaded. It is becoming very difficult to see what is gained by trying to fit all the complex post-war developments into a conceptual frame that must be so loose and clumsy as to be virtually worthless— except, perhaps, as a vague, emotive symbol.

The point is heavily underlined by the post-war history of the communist movement. While it was dominated by Stalin, it had a monolithic unity: dissenters were expelled (or, within the USSR, purged), and communists all over the world accepted the 'leading role' of the Soviet party, which became the arbiter of theoretical and tactical issues. This Soviet primacy was the corollary of the doctrine of 'socialism in one country'; while there was only one communist state, there was only one official brand of communism. Step by step, however, it became more difficult for the Soviet Union to maintain this position. There were, first of all, the new communist régimes in East Europe—set up, it is true, under Soviet tutelage by party leaders who had been schooled under Stalinism—whose history and social structures differed from that of Russia. The strains that resulted from the attempt to impose the Soviet pattern on them led to the anti-Soviet outbreaks in Hungary and Poland in 1956. Even before that date, moreover, there had been the sensational breakaway of the Tito régime in Yugoslavia. In 1948, at the moment that the Stalinists were taking over in most of East Europe, the one communist régime that had achieved its own revolution in the course of the war refused to accept Stalin's policies and set out to prove that 'independent' communism was doctrinally and politically possible. In the same year, the Chinese communists had also come to power by their own efforts, and with policies that markedly differed from those of Soviet communism—though the differences were soft-pedalled, in the name of communist unity, until by 1960 it became impossible to conceal them.

Stalin died in 1953. By 1956, his successor Nikita Krushchev was already speaking of 'different roads to socialism' in an attempt to find a formula which would permit communist parties to adapt themselves to varying conditions while retaining some common front in foreign affairs. By 1960, when representatives of eighty-one communist parties met in Moscow to draw up a 'new' Communist Manifesto, there was a final effort to write a general declaration of policy to which all could subscribe; but the document produced was so ambiguous and contradictory that it had no practical value other than serving as the last attempt to glass over the profound divergence between Moscow and Peking. Since then, the once-monolithic communist movement has broken up, and its component parts lack any common view of what constitutes a Marxist ideology in the modern world or of what form a 'socialist' society should take. The doctrine of 'polycentrism', which has replaced Stalinism, means little more than that the communist régimes maintain a loose alliance for the purposes of survival while choosing the internal policies which suit their own political purposes. Chinese denunciations of 'revisionism' in the Soviet Union, and in all the European communist parties with the exception of isolated and backward Albania, are quite as fierce as any of the polemics which Stalinists once directed against social-democrats.

For all these reasons it is hard to write a coherent or chronological account of the changes in socialism since 1945. Unless one accepts the simple and unconvincing claim of the Chinese communists and their supporters that they are the true heirs of the classical socialist movement, and that all others are no more than overt or covert sympathisers with bourgeois imperialism, it is necessary to concede that this movement no longer exists. We may use the word 'socialism' in a general sense, to distinguish certain types of doctrine from, for instance, liberal individualism or clerical authoritarianism, just as we use the term 'Christianity' to mark off one form of religious belief from Mahommedanism or Judaism. But in the same way as the serious student of Christianity analyses Roman Catholicism, Methodism or the Plymouth Brethren, as a specific belief held in specific historical circumstances, the student of socialism must examine Russian or Chinese communism, Algerian or Ghanaian socialism, or British social-democracy as historically specific phenomena.

The reader of this book may begin this task by turning to the volumes recommended for further reading, which contain essential documents and detailed commentaries on events since 1945. But, as an epilogue to the history summarised in these pages, it may be useful to note a few of these developments.

In terms of numbers, and of world politics, it is of course clear that the most dramatic developments in the last two decades have been the growth and transformation of the communist movement. Yet, if we consider the various movements that arose from the development of capitalism in the nineteenth century, we shall see that the one which remains closest to them in form and outlook is the British Labour Party. It was always, with its base in the trade unions, one of the strongest of the social-democratic parties, though with its beliefs heavily tinged by religious dissent it never absorbed more than the most general propositions of Marxism. (Much the same is true of the other social-democratic parties—in Scandinavia, Australia and New Zealand—that have been able to maintain themselves successfully all through this century.) It has remained the one party which, in a major industrial country, not only accepts the traditional socialist critique of capitalism but also continues to assert that a socialist society can be established by democratic means. Other social-democratic parties survive (in Belgium, France, West Germany, Austria and Italy, for example), but all of them have suffered more vicissitudes than the Labour Party. Some, as in France, lost out in the competition with the communists or, as with the Nenni socialists in Italy, found it necessary to maintain a loose alliance with them; others, as in Holland and Austria, have moved in and out of coalitions with democratic Catholic parties; and though the Social Democrats are the main opposition in West Germany, they have so revised their policies that they must be regarded as a movement of moderate social reform, enjoying trade union support, rather than as even a nominally socialist party.

In Britain, however, Labour was distinguished by winning power by electoral means—the only large socialist party ever to achieve this, and thus to provide apparent proof that the classical socialist assumptions were valid. Yet the experience of the Labour government which came to power in 1945 suggests that while the reform of capitalism may be desirable and possible by democratic means, its replacement by a different social system may be less easy; and the point is underlined by the election of yet another Labour administration, led by Harold Wilson, in 1964. Twenty years after Clement Attlee won his dramatic victory, Britain has brought about one-fifth of the economy under public ownership, introduced a welfare state, stepped up taxation on both inherited and acquired wealth, accepted a substantial amount of economic planning both by direct and fiscal measures—yet has retained a dominant private sector in industry, and done relatively little to rectify striking inequalities of property and opportunity. Britain remains a class society, and one in which it is still possible for the Conservative and Labour parties to alternate in office without dramatic reversals of policy.

This was not what had been expected in 1945. Labour's election manifesto, *Let Us Face the Future*, had set out a programme of nationalisation and social welfare which was widely regarded as the first instalment of socialism. But while these measures, combined with economic policies designed to restore Britain's war-stricken industry and trade, helped put the country on its feet and provide a greater measure of social security, they did not radically change Britain's social structure nor introduce policies which were wholly unacceptable to private enterprise or its political champion, the Conservative Party. True, on regaining office in 1951, the Conservatives denationalised the steel and road haulage industries, and made changes in the taxation system which reduced its redistributive effect, but otherwise they left Labour's reforms essentially untouched. The main features of a mixed economy, with a commitment to a welfare state, had become common ground between the parties.

There are grounds for believing that a system of this kind is a logical product of advanced capitalism. There are, naturally, great political differences between, say, Britain, France, the United States and Japan; but it is remarkable that, socially speaking, they have come to resemble each other very closely. All of them have a degree of state ownership and control in a society predominantly based on private enterprise; all of them have extensive welfare provisions; all of them permit a wide range of political opinions and activity; all of them permit trade union organisation and free collective bargaining —and the same is true of Canada, Australia, the Scandinavian countries, Switzerland, the Low Countries, Austria and Italy. Though the British Labour Party may see itself as a socialist party, its practical effect may not differ substantially from the results achieved in countries where quite different agencies have secured comparable reforms.

For this reason there is no need to examine in detail the policies followed by the Labour government after 1945, or the new programme *Socialism for the Sixties* on which Labour won the 1964 election, as if they contained unique proposals for transforming capitalism. It seems that they are essentially minor variations on a major theme which is common to all industrial democracies. We should, however, note that many members of the Labour Party have not seen things in quite this light. In 1945, they believed they were moving towards a socialist society; in 1964, they continued to assert that this was their ultimate objective; and in between, they were engaged in a long and disruptive controversy about this very point. Was the Labour Party socialist? And, if so, what did socialism mean in Britain in the middle of the twentieth century?

These questions had already been raised before the Attlee government had completed its term of office—though they were first directed at issues of foreign policy. The years of the Popular Front, and of wartime collaboration with the Soviet Union, had made their mark on the active membership of the Labour Party. A substantial part of the membership not only regarded itself as socialist in domestic affairs; it was also sympathetic to the USSR, and inclined to suspect the United States of reactionary and even imperialist objectives. The fact that the Labour government had depended upon a sizeable American loan intensified rather than diminished these feelings. In the earliest phase of the Cold War, the Labour Left-wingers had called for 'a socialist foreign policy' (by which they meant a more conciliatory policy towards the Soviet Union and communist régimes in Europe) and opposed American anti-communist policies. By 1951, the political consequences of the Korean War had intensified this tendency; the economic consequences, exaggerated by a large rearmament programme, had led to the defeat of the Labour Party and the return of the Conservatives.

Against this background, a new radical agitation began in the Labour Party, under the leadership of Aneurin Bevan and Harold Wilson, who had resigned from the Attlee government before its defeat in opposition to the policy of rearmament. This agitation, broadly known as the Bevanite movement, persisted up to 1959; its main objectives were a more socialist domestic programme and a foreign policy which broke away from the leadership of Washington. It was especially opposed to 'nuclear diplomacy', and many of its supporters eventually focussed their energies on the Campaign for Nuclear Disarmament, which called for Britain's unilateral renunciation of atomic weapons. The movement was influential: at the peak of its strength it was able, in 1960, to carry Labour's national conference with it by a narrow majority. But with the successive deaths of Aneurin Bevan and Hugh Gaitskell—who had succeeded Clement Attlee as leader of the party—and the emergence of Harold

Wilson as party leader, this Left-wing agitation subsided. It left its mark on Labour policy; but the long debate had done little more than give a fresh airing to a dilemma that had always confronted Labour. Left-wing socialists might be able to dominate the party organisation in the country, and write radical measures into its programme. But the party could win an election only by stressing its moderation. This ambivalence, important in opposition, becomes more critical when a Labour government takes office. As the first months of Harold Wilson's administration showed, it has to satisfy its supporters that it has socialist intentions; but it also has to avoid drastic interference with business interests and domestic policies that might destroy foreign confidence in the pound. If it fails in the first objective, it is liable to disruption, as Bevanism demonstated; if it fails in the second, it may be faced with a disastrous crisis of confidence in the economy.

From the standpoint of the sociologist, who can observe how a social-democratic movement of this kind gradually modifies an industrial society, and popularises reforms to a point where even a Conservative government can assimilate them, it may not greatly matter that such a dilemma cannot be resolved. It may well be argued that it has played a valuable part in British life. The existence of the Labour Party may have provided an instrument through which new ideas are injected into British public life, and a means whereby the working-class has been given a substantial stake in national affairs. But, to the committed socialist, such an opinion smacks of heresy. For a variety of reasons, some social and some psychological, he believes in the vision of the New Jerusalem, and he judges Labour policy by the degree to which it appears to be building that new society. He is, in a curious way, deeply conservative, clinging strongly to attitudes formed more than half a century ago, an endeavouring to make a nineteenth-century ideology fit twentieth-century facts.

It was such a contrast that led some members of the Labour Party to attempt to revise the fundamental assumptions of the party, and specifically (in 1959) to propose the abolition of Clause Four of its constitution, which calls in the traditional fashion for the 'common ownership of the means of production, distribution and exchange'. A clear statement of the revisionist position was made by Anthony Crosland, in *The Future of Socialism*; but though, in practical terms, revisionist policies were adopted by the Wilson government, doctrinally it proved impossible to persuade the party to give up its cherished socialist principles.

The Labour Party was not the only organisation to find difficulty in matching old doctrines to new situations. Its difficulties were trivial compared with those which afflicted the communist movement in the post-war years.

For a time, after the war ended, Stalin was able to maintain the established pattern of Soviet orthodoxy. Through the worst years of the Cold War, from 1948 to 1953, the same terror, the same labour camps, and the same pressure on the peasantry were used to rebuild the Soviet economy that had been employed to create it in the 'thirties. The results were remarkable. By the time Stalin died, Soviet industry had reached a high technical level, capable of nuclear energy, space rocketry and other complex products, though housing, food and consumer goods remained in short supply. What was equally remarkable, in a different sense, was Stalin's success in imposing precise copies of the Soviet system on the satellite régimes of East Europe. Each was given a heavy industrial base; each was forced to collectivise agriculture; each copied administrative details down to police methods, and even to the design of signs on shops. Regardless of separate national traditions, each country was forced as far as possible into an identical mould. Lip-service was paid to the idea that these People's Democracies had a 'new road' to socialism, and it was argued that they would be able—thanks to the destruction of the old régimes in war and to the aid of the Soviet Union—to proceed to the establishment of socialism without an intervening period of bourgeois democracy. But this 'revolution from above' was nothing more than the forced adoption of the Stalinist model of socialism. Any attempt to differ from this model led, as in the case of Yugoslavia, to expulsion from the communist fold, or to draconian purges for 'nationalist deviation'; the years after 1948 were punctuated by show trials of communists who failed to follow Stalin's line in any respect.

By 1953, however, this line was patently failing to work. Soviet society had reached a point of complexity where it could no longer be ruled by the crude techniques that had done service during the 'thirties; to develop, it needed more flexibility internally, just as it needed to escape from the difficulties created in foreign affairs by Stalin's intransigent tactics. In the satellite régimes, popular dissatisfaction was growing; the communist rulers survived because the Soviet army underwrote their power, but collectivisation had worked no better for them than it had in Russia, and industrialisation was creating a new class of workers who were as exploited and restless as the proletariat of Western countries in the time of Marx. Yugoslavia and China were following independent policies; and the communist movement elsewhere had achieved nothing from its 'hard' line in the Cold War but isolation and defeat. Stalinist orthodoxy still claimed to be Marxist: theoretically and practically it had run into a dead end.

From 1948, the Yugoslav communists had been making significant revisions in that orthodoxy, to the accompaniement of fierce denunciations by Moscow which probably served more to publicise the revisionist heresy than to combat it. In 1955, Stalin's successor, Nikita Krushchev, made the first dramatic break with the past; he flew to Belgrade, admitted the 'errors' Stalin had made, and called off the campaign against the Tito régime. A few months later, the Soviet communists met for their 20th Party Congress, and heard Krushchev deliver (in secret, but the text became available in a short time) a speech which catalogued the crimes of Stalinism. This speech left much obscure and unsaid, and concentrated upon Stalin's terror against loyal communists rather than upon the more fundamental failures of his régime, but it confirmed a good deal that Trotskyists and other anti-Stalinists had argued for years—down to precise details of the purges, and Stalin's destruction of the old revolutionary élite in Russia.

The effect of this speech was staggering. By confirming much that had hitherto been surmised about Stalinism, it disrupted the whole communist movement. At the same time, Krushchev's revelations seemed to promise an era of reform, in which differences of opinion would not invite the attention of the secret police, and a new attempt could be made to build a socialist society closer to the original Marxist model. Krushchev, for doctrinal reasons, continually urged a return to the Leninist 'norms' which Stalin had violated; but he had become, in fact, the leading revisionist. A glance at the *New Programme* of the Communist Party of the Soviet Union, published in November 1961 after a complex debate on de-Stalinisation during the previous five years, shows how tortuously the new leadership was trying to reconcile what had been achieved under Stalin with what clearly needed to be done before the Soviet Union became recognisably socialist in the traditional sense.

A shock of this kind may have been necessary to shake Russia out of the Stalinist strait-jacket. But it was so powerful that it almost shook East Europe out of the Soviet sphere, and did begin the process of alienation from China. Krushchev's speech had a popular effect: all over the communist world there was an outbreak of revisionist ideas, in which communists began to re-read Marx, and to discover how far Lenin and Stalin had diverged from his original conceptions. But, at the same time, the Soviet leaders were putting pressure on the satellite régimes to reform themselves before unrest swept them away. This pressure, however, made these régimes even more uncertain and shaky. Dramatic de-Stalinisation might be possible in the Soviet Union, where forty years of isolation and dictatorship had removed any real alternative to a communist régime. It was a very risky business in the régimes of East Europe. For one thing, the Soviet leaders could appeal back from Stalin to a Leninist legitimacy; creatures of Stalin, they could shrug off some of the responsibility for what had happened by claiming that they too were under police terror, and win popular support by promising that the old evils would not recur. But the satellite politicians had no such recourse. They were Stalin's men, hand-picked; it was Stalin's army that had enabled them to disrupt the post-war coalitions in East Europe and impose Stalin's style of communism. If Stalin were repudiated, how could they survive? If proletarian internationalism (the communist jargon for support from the Soviet army) were abandoned, what was to hold the incipient nationalism of their countries in check? With the exception of the Poles, who had only imprisoned and not shot 'national communist' factions, the satellite parties did not even have strong alternative leaders, free of the Stalinist taint, who could be resurrected in this crisis.

It was the survival of Wladislaw Gomulka, former secretary of the Polish communists, which probably prevented the collapse of the Polish régime. Revisionism went further in Poland than elsewhere; so did a deep sense of nationalism and widespread adherence to the Catholic Church. By a series of desperate manœuvres, which involved the threat of armed defiance of the Russians and the reorganisation of both the leadership and the policy of the Polish Workers' Party, Gomulka harnessed the 'Polish Revolution', as it was widely styled, to a peaceful though compromise solution. Poland was to follow its own road to socialism, remaining within the communist camp but abandoning the worst features of Stalinism—including the collectivisation of the land.

Hungary was less fortunate. It had a possible leader in Imre Nagy, who had already emerged in the years after Stalin's death as the protagonist of a 'new course'; but in Rakosi and Gero, who had retained effective control, it had two of the most despotic and inflexible Stalinists in Europe. Even the party intellectuals had become openly hostile to the régime, and they provided a focus for the discontent of the workers and peasants. In 1956, in the name of 'genuine socialism', they rose against the régime and destroyed it within a few days.

The subsequent story is well known: the Soviet army, after an initial withdrawal, returned after Imre Nagy had permitted the formation of bourgeois parties, proclaimed Hungary's neutrality and had withdrawn from the Warsaw Pact; the revolution was suppressed and a new communist régime led by Janos Kadar was installed. But it is an important story, because the Hungarian revolution in some ways came closer to Marx's original model than any event before or since. Ironically, it took place in a nominally communist country. But it conformed to all the 'material preconditions' Marx had set out, save one. Industry was not owned by an exploiting capitalist class; it was, however, controlled by a bureaucratic clique which behaved like a ruling class with monopolistic rights over the economy—and over the state machine as a whole. In other respects the comparison is close. There was an exploited proletariat, a dissatisfied intelligentsia, and a depressed peasantry. There was concentration of industry, economic stagnation, and a falling standard of life. Above all (in the Marxist texts that the régime had religously disseminated) there was available a revolutionary ideology which could be used to mobilise the will to change. But it is evidence of its genuinely revolutionary character that all its essential demands—save formal recognition of other political parties and withdrawal from the alliance with the USSR—have been accepted as a necessary part of 'Hungarian socialism' by the Kadar régime.

In the subsequent ten years, de-Stalinisation has followed a chequered course in East Europe and in the USSR. There has been some liberalisation, a relaxation of the strict Stalinist policies in matters of culture, a more conciliatory attitude towards neutral and even capitalist states. It has even become possible for fairly large numbers of western tourists to enter the communist countries—a point on which Stalin was so sensitive that visitors were restricted to hand-picked 'delegations'. We cannot discuss these events in detail, nor can we examine the ideological complexities of Marxist revisionism. Both subjects really lie beyond the scope of this book.

We must, nevertheless, make one general point about the changes that have taken place in Russia and East Europe since Stalin's death. They all amount to a decline in both orthodoxy and militancy; and with this decline the régimes seem to have gained greater stability. It would be saying too much if we suggested that they were becoming popular—in the sense that any communist régime could win an election. But they have become much more flexible, more sensitive to shifts in public opinion, more willing to tolerate dissent.

It is precisely such changes that have aroused the ire of the Chinese, who regard this process as a betrayal of socialism brought about by the cowardice and muddle-headedness of Krushchev and his associates. From 1957 in private, from 1960 in public, the Chinese have quarrelled with every aspect of Soviet policy. They have objected to de-Stalinisation, to Krushchev's insistence on the need, in a nuclear age, for peaceful co-existence between different social systems, to Soviet support for bourgeois nationalists (such as Nehru and Nasser), to Russian attempts to reach any understanding with the United States, to the tactics of the French and Italian communists, to Soviet relations with Yugoslavia, to developments in East Europe, to Soviet reluctance to give adequate support to North Vietnam and to Cuba in their conflicts with the USA, and above all to Soviet failure to give China either the nuclear or the economic aid that Peking wished.

It is easy to write off the Chinese communists as unrepentant Stalinists: in their dogmatism, and their suspicion of dissenters, and their emphasis on building industry on the Stalinist model, there is much to justify the comparison. But there is also a Trotskyist touch to their messianic belief in the revolution. They have effectively written off the Russians, much as Lenin once wrote off the Second International; and with the Russians they have also dismissed most of the communists in the advanced countries. The true believer today, they argue, turns to Peking rather than Moscow, is prepared for armed struggle against imperialism, throws in his lot with the poor peasants of Asia, Africa, and Latin America, and is not terrified into 'capitulationism' by the nuclear strength of Western imperialism. Chinese communists have even argued that a Third World War would end with the universal triumph of communism; it might indeed if the West and Russia used their massive nuclear strength against each other, and the hundreds of millions of peasants survived, under Chinese leadership, to inherit the earth.

But one can see why, when the Soviet Union is at last approaching something like economic and military comparability with the West, such militant doctrines should prove unappealing. What could the Soviet Union gain today by engaging in open hostility to the United States, by diverting resources and political energy to promoting peasant wars all round the globe, by imposing a new ideological corset on its own people and on those of East Europe? Would such a policy serve Soviet interests—even though it might square more easily with the orthodox communist doctrines to which the Chinese subscribe?

After nearly fifty years of hardship and dictatorship, the Soviet Union is slowly feeling its way towards a different type of society— certainly one based upon public ownership of the means of production, distribution and exchange, and possibly closer to western conceptions of what socialism should mean in terms of human dignity and freedom. What shape that society will assume cannot be predicted, any more than the precise events that followed the death of Stalin were predictable. But it is emerging as a result of industrialisation, the growth of cities, the appearance of new social strata of managers, technicians and professionals, the need for peace and economic growth.

China is still far from the point where such a development could occur. Apart from the ideological commitment to a revolutionary policy, and to the support of every anti-imperialist movement in every under-developed country—a commitment which inevitably has 'anti-white' racialist undertones—its leaders have still to achieve the transformation of the largest peasant society on earth into a viable modern economy. The attempt to short-circuit the process of 'establishing socialism' by setting up peasant communes was far from successful, and one of the causes of friction with the Soviet Union; the hope of using the resources of the Soviet Union to speed up the process of industrialisation was also disappointed. Add to this China's different political traditions, and her long isolation from the outside world—an isolation perpetuated by her exclusion from the United Nations and her non-recognition by the United States—and it is clear that, for many years to come, Chinese communism will be a dynamic and difficult element in world politics.

There is a long and intricate history which links Marx, the young Hegelian democrat, with Mao Tse-tung or the Vietcong guerilla. Whether the line of descent is legitimate matters less than the fact that it is felt to be a genuine revolutionary inheritance, and all of us —American democrats, British social-democrats, Russian communists, African neutralists—have to live with that fact.

This book began by noting the revolutionary impact of the ideas of the French Revolution and the machinery of the industrial revolution. They produced bourgeois capitalism, and its response— the socialism and the trade union movement of the nineteenth century. They produced in the setting of Russia, the breakdown of Tsarist autocracy, and its response—Leninist communism. In Asia, Africa and Latin America they produced imperialism, and its response—a radical nationalism. Somewhere, in each of these movements, there lies the idea that man can enjoy liberty, equality and fraternity, and that the machine may provide him with the material means to these moral ends. Through the defeats, the mistakes, the terror and the tragedy, that idea keeps alive—and it is the central idea of socialism.

FURTHER READING

Most libraries will contain volumes on the development of socialist theory and organisation, especially on Marxist ideas and the subsequent communist movement. But a number of useful works, which will serve as supplements to this book, are now available in British or American paperbacks. The list given below is not exclusive: some will pass out of print while new titles are added. A glance at the catalogue of paperbacks in print, which can be consulted at any good bookstore, will be helpful. Readers should look under the appropriate headings, such as Socialism, Communism, Soviet Union, China, Politics, Philosophy, History, Trade Unionism and Economics.

A group of three books will provide some historical background. *The Pursuit of the Millenium* (Harper) by Norman Cohn deals with messianic revolutionary movements; *The Origins of Totalitarian Democracy* (Mercury) by J. Talmon examines the Jacobin tradition; and *Anatomy of Revolution* (Vintage) by Crane Brinton looks for common patterns in the American, French and Russian Revolutions. Further reading on imaginary societies (not all of which are socialist) can be found in an anthology entitled *The Quest for Utopia* (Anchor) which is edited by Glenn Negley and J. Max Patrick.

Other helpful anthologies may be consulted. *Socialist Thought* (Anchor) is edited by A. Fried and R. Sanders; *Marx and Engels: Basic Writings on Politics and Philosophy* (Anchor) is edited by

L. S. Feuer; *The Marxists* (Dell) is edited with comments by C. Wright Mills; and *The Essential Works of Marxism* (Bantam Classic) is edited by Arthur P. Mendel. The last of these contains extracts from writings by the Yugoslav revisionist Milovan Djilas, and the Polish revisionist Laszek Kolakowski, as well as Marx, Engels, Lenin, Stalin and Mao Tse-tung.

E. Fromm has written an introduction to an edition of some of Marx's earliest writings which express his theory of alienation, published as *Marx's Concept of Man* (Ungar). F. Schumpeter's *Capitalism, Socialism and Democracy* (Harper) is a standard text, which compares Marxism with other modern socialist theories. *Marxism* (Praeger) by George Lichtheim is a general but stimulating commentary. *The New Communist Manifesto* (Harper) edited by Dan N. Jacobs not only reprints the original manifesto of 1848 but also contains a helpful collection of recent documents, such as Krushchev's secret speech of 1956, various documents of the international communist gatherings after 1956, and the new programme of the CPSU. For the earlier period of Marxism and the nineteenth-century labour movement, see also *Anarchism* (Meridian) by George Woodcock.

A. Meyer's *Leninism* (Praeger) is a good introduction. Leon Trotsky's *The Revolution Betrayed* (Pioneer) and Rosa Luxemburg's *The Russian Revolution* (Ann Arbor) are important original polemical tracts. A more recent polemic against communist bureaucracy, also written by a revisionist, is *The New Class* (Praeger) by Milovan Djilas.

There are many books on the Soviet system itself. John N. Hazard's *The Soviet System of Government* (Chicago) and *How The Soviet System Works* (Vintage) by R. A. Bauer, A. Inkeles and C. Kluckhohn are useful introductions. On the communist régimes in East Europe, see H. Seton Watson's *The East European Revolution* (Praeger) and S. Fisher-Galati, *Eastern Europe in the Sixties* (Praeger). Many aspects of Marxist revisionism, with special attention to the ideas and events of 1956, are well discussed in the symposium

Revisionism (Praeger), which is edited by L. Labedz. *The Dilemma of Democratic Socialism* (Collier) by Peter Gay is a stimulating exposition of the views of the first important revisionist, Eduard Bernstein. The text of Bernstein's own classic, *Evolutionary Socialism* (Schocken), is also available. The Sino-Soviet dispute is dealt with in David Floyd's *Mao Against Krushchev* (Praeger) and in Edward Crankshaw's *The New Cold War* (Penguin). For essential and not otherwise easily accessible texts of Chinese communist leaders, see John Wilson Lewis, *Major Doctrines of Communist China* (Norton).

On British social-democracy, Anthony Crosland's *The Future of Socialism* (Schocken) is essential reading. Margaret Cole's *The Story of Fabian Socialism* (Mercury) deals with the earlier period.

INDEX